TEN WAYS OF
ABOUT SAMU
THE FALSETT

Enoch Brater is the Kenneth T. Rowe Collegiate Professor of Dramatic Literature at the University of Michigan. He has published widely in the field of modern drama, and is an internationally renowned expert on such figures as Samuel Beckett and Arthur Miller. His seminal studies on Beckett include *Beyond Minimalism: Beckett's Late Style in the Theater* (Oxford University Press, 1987); *The Drama in the Text: Beckett's Late Fiction* (Oxford University Press, 1994); *Beckett at 80/Beckett in Context* (Oxford University Press, 1986); and *The Essential Samuel Beckett* (Thames & Hudson, 2005).

TEN WAYS OF THINKING ABOUT SAMUEL BECKETT: THE FALSETTO OF REASON

Enoch Brater

Methuen Drama

Methuen Drama

1 3 5 7 9 10 8 6 4 2

First published in Great Britain in 2011 by Methuen Drama

Methuen Drama, an imprint of Bloomsbury Publishing Plc

Methuen Drama
Bloomsbury Publishing Plc
36 Soho Square
London W1D 3QY
www.methuendrama.com

ISBN 978 1 408 13722 2

Available in the USA from Bloomsbury Academic & Professional,
175 Fifth Avenue /3rd Floor, New York, NY10010
www.BloomsburyAcademicUSA.com

A CIP catalogue record for this book is available from the British Library

Typeset by Country Setting, Kingsdown, Kent
Printed and bound in Great Britain by CPI Cox & Wyman,
Reading, Berkshire

Caution

For Hersh, Toby, Linda, Porter, Toñi and Stan

CONTENTS

Clov No one that ever lived thought as crooked as we.

Hamm We do what we can.

Endgame

PREFACE

Beckett and a Way of Thinking

'Beckett is the last writer to shape the way we think and feel.'
Don DeLillo, *Mao II*

In one of those great passages from the novel *Molloy*, the kind that reminds you why you read Beckett in the first place, the storytelling, such as it is, is abruptly stopped in its tracks when a Keatsian reminiscence of things recently past oddly intrudes:

> Do you know what he told me the other day . . . He said to me, said Gaber, Gaber, he said—. Louder! I cried. He said to me, said Gaber, Gaber, he said, life is a thing of beauty, Gaber, and a joy for ever . . . A joy for ever, he said, a thing of beauty, Moran, and a joy for ever . . . I said, Do you think he meant human life?[1]

The intercalated dialogue, all talk (like the rest of the fictional enterprise), is of course part of the storytelling too. But it is just as telling in other ways as well, ways that go to the heart of the matter concerning Beckett's accomplishment in terms of big-ticket items like *being* and *representation*, and remind us even more forcefully why there continues to be so many ways of thinking about his work as playwright, novelist and poet. That Beckett is a writer's writer is by this date hardly what anyone would call big news, nor did he need the Nobel Prize Committee in Stockholm to validate his status as such in 1969. The tributes in this regard are as legendary as they are sometimes surprising: among fellow dramatists, Harold Pinter,

Edward Albee, Sam Shepard, David Mamet, Tom Stoppard, Vaclav Havel and even Lillian Hellman have said in one way or another how profoundly influenced they were by everything he wrote. That holds true for Arthur Miller too, the un-Beckett, who admitted late in life that 'that man was up to something'.[2] And yet, strange as it may seem, there are no 'sons of Sam'. In this 'case nought' the influence is more difficult to track and trace, but just as assuredly all-encompassing.

What Beckett's legacy may be finally about is what I like to call 'a way of thinking'. And that way of thinking should be already apparent in the short passage cited above. No's knife is everywhere in yes's wound, placed there in something like safe keeping. Keep me in mind, the passage seems to say, keep me in mind for when you need me most, on the next rainy day perhaps, or even more so in the 'world without end'. Moran's is not a throwaway line; it's offered to us, instead, as though it were some sort of final prayer at last: the one that asks for nothing. And like all great masters, Beckett is both an artist representative of his time and one who stands apart from it. (I know we're not supposed to talk about 'great masters' any more, but what are you supposed to do with Beckett? Subject him to 'commodification' and say 'that's it'?)

Let's take a close look at what a few lines from Beckett's fiction can do. Postmodern before they may have been quite ready to be *post-*, they tell us, among other things, how a writer deals with a profoundly romantic sense of loss when his audience can no longer take its anxiety and avidity raw. Irony reigns, and it cuts deep, but it does so, at best, only tenuously: something of all that misery remains. 'Endymion' is recycled in the only way this sort of lyricism can now be recaptured – recuperated really – in spite of and surely *because of* the fact that Keats now has a dirty finger in his eye. How ironic. How romantic. How Beckettian, really – and it's not every writer who gets his name turned into such a weighty adjective. That's not moving, that's *moving*.[3]

Conscious of his literary past, but never for one moment cowed by it, as no real writer ever is, Beckett seems to have known from the start that having something to say could never be separated from his own way of saying *it*, 'not knowing what'. *Saying* was only *inventing* anyway, 'rhetorical question less the rhetoric'. After Joyce, after Yeats, after Proust and even, yes, after his beloved Dante, '*Simile qui con simile è sepolto*' – like with like is buried here. What Beckett's writing gives us, finally, he perhaps said best himself, solo, in *Ohio Impromptu*: 'Thoughts, no, not thoughts. Profounds of mind.'[4]

The chapters that follow offer Beckett's reader, more often his theatre audience, an opportunity to consider his work from a variety of sometimes 'demented' perspectives. Eccentric at times, they aim to suggest new ways of thinking about Beckett's own way of thinking. Beginning with a re-view of his signature work, *Waiting for Godot* – 'no longer merely a play', as the director Alan Schneider pointed out, but 'a condition of life', even, perhaps, a state of mind – this discussion aims to display a panorama of words and images reworked and expanded, returned and refreshed by what Molloy calls 'the falsetto of reason', and also to show that every way of thinking about Beckett is an invitation to 'fail again', only to 'fail better'.[5]

CHAPTER 1

Things to Ponder while Waiting for Godot

Samuel Beckett's most famous play, *Waiting for Godot*, begins with one character sitting on a low mound struggling to take off a boot, and ends when two tramps threaten to walk off the set but don't: '*They do not move.*'[1] There's more to it than that, of course, but that's about it, as Didi and Gogo struggle to pass the time of day anticipating the arrival of a central personality clad in mystery and myth, an offstage operative who never appears. A lot happens in between, including the transit of two other figures, Pozzo and Lucky – twice, though this work seems bent on reminding us from the very outset that there's 'Nothing to be done.' Gogo's opening line, which sets this refrain of entropy ironically and energetically in motion, will be repeated no less than three times in the spirited dialogue written for the first of the drama's two acts. Those fateful four words have been the subject of so much critical commentary, as has the play itself, that it is sometimes difficult to keep in mind that *Godot* was composed as an exercise in extreme economy of mood and atmosphere and gesture, a dogged enterprise in transforming the simple act of waiting into the entirety of the dramatic enterprise itself. Godot doesn't come, but Beckett's characters never give up on him, or on one another. When the moon rises, artificial yet real, and night falls on this minimalist stage set, we suddenly know what they already know: that they will be back waiting for their man tomorrow. 'That's how it is on this bitch of an earth.'

Beckett wrote his landmark play in French in 1949 and called it *En attendant Godot* (the translation we read in English is his own). Roger Blin's premiere production four years later at the Théâtre de Babylone on the boulevard Raspail in Paris ran for more than a hundred performances and was generally well received by the daily newspaper critics, as well as by those writing more considered pieces for the monthly magazines.[2] The playwright quickly asserted his authority over *Godot* and its staggering symmetry by matching a minimum of plot with a minimum of stage scenery: a mound, a moon and a bare tree sprouting a few unexpected leaves for the opening of the second act, where Didi sings his song about a dog, a kitchen and a misbegotten loaf of bread.

There is a similar rationing of props; Gogo and Didi, more elegantly known as Estragon and Vladimir, may wear cast-off formal attire and sport bowler hats that have seen better days, but they must nonetheless make do with radishes, turnips and one pitiful carrot. Boots, on the other hand, come in for special treatment in terms of size and fit and colour, and there is more than one pair of them. Pozzo brings to this uneasy display some welcome 'reinforcements', including a whip, a rope, an aspirator and a watch (some of these items mysteriously disappear), while his servant Lucky, a 'knook' who 'carries like a pig', is burdened with suitcases, a stool and a picnic basket with a few snacks of chicken: 'The fresh air stimulates the jaded appetite.' Even Beckett's characters despair of the limited threshold assigned to them. Stage life's tough, and they know they're really down on their luck when they haven't even got 'a good bit of rope' with which to hang themselves (would-be 'erections' must consequently be postponed):

Vladimir Charming evening we're having.

Estragon Unforgettable.

Vladimir And it's not over yet.

Estragon Apparently not.

Vladimir It's only beginning.

Estragon It's awful.

> **Vladimir** Worse than the pantomime.
> **Estragon** The circus.
> **Vladimir** The music-hall.
> **Estragon** The circus.

Waiting for Godot firmly establishes Beckett's credentials as a playwright determined to do more and more on stage with less and less – an aesthetic he will raise to unpredictable heights as his drama matures, develops and retracts. The achievement is all the more impressive in that he began writing plays as 'a relaxation', to get away from 'the awful prose' he was working on at the time. 'I needed a habitable space,' he said, 'and I found it on the stage.'[3] *Godot*, is, however, anything but an afterthought; indeed, it might be hard to imagine what theatre in the western world would look like today without its profound impact on nothing less than the dramatic imagination itself.

That is making a rather large claim for Beckett's play. Yet *Waiting for Godot*, as it brings new life to the theatre, early on reveals the scope of its ambition. Even the names Beckett assigns to his principal characters extend the range of representation to encompass, as the dialogue boldly states, 'all humanity', at least in its recognisably European variety: Slavic Vladimir, French Estragon, Italian Pozzo, English Lucky. In the lined student notebook Beckett used to write this play Vladimir (Didi) was originally called Lèvy, a Jewish name loaded with disturbing resonances in this post-Holocaust landscape; the playwright said Pozzo's carrier was 'perhaps' called Lucky because, in a world like this, 'he had no more expectations'.[4] Not surprisingly, 'Godot' has been far more difficult to pin down. Although his name has been considered as a bilingual pun on fundamentals like God and water (French *eau*), his patrimony continues to resist any neat system of synchronisation. 'I . . . seem never to have had the least faculty or disposition for the supernatural,' Beckett wrote in an early letter. And in another:

'There may be Gods, but what ice do they cut?' When asked on more than one occasion, 'Who or what is Godot?' the playwright replied, 'If I knew, I would have said so in the play.'[5]

The same ambiguity and the same quest for certainty extend to almost every element in the work's borderline inscrutability. We are rather in the position of Tantalus, as Beckett observed early on in his essay on Proust, but with one crucial difference: and that is that in the theatre we 'allow ourselves to be tantalised'.[6] Access, apparently encouraged, goes only so far. Biblical references, for example, abound, but they don't necessarily take us where we think they might go. Vladimir initiates a pattern of specifically Christian allusion with a perceptive close reading of the Gospels: why is it that only 'one of the four' reports that only 'one of the two' was saved, cross-checking as he does the textual evidence relating to the two thieves summarily crucified with the so-said 'Saviour' in the so-said 'Holy Land'.

> And yet . . . (*pause*) . . . how is it – this is not boring you
> I hope – how is it that of the four Evangelists only one
> speaks of a thief being saved. The four of them were there –
> or thereabouts – and only one speaks of a thief being
> saved . . . One out of four. Of the other three two don't
> mention any thieves at all and the third says that both of
> them abused him . . . all four were there. And only one
> speaks of a thief being saved. Why believe him rather than
> the others?

Beckett's wayfarers draw different conclusions in the face of hermeneutic uncertainty. While Didi says he's more or less content with a 50–50 crack at redemption – 'a reasonable percentage', after all – Gogo's response to the popular tale of the thief Barabbas's good fortune may be far more unsettling: 'People are bloody ignorant apes.' Theirs is an 'absolute absence of the absolute'.[7]

All but the most literary in Beckett's audience will miss the double-barrelled allusion in Gogo's throwaway line, 'The wind in the reeds' (a homage to William Butler Yeats as well as to the *Gospel According to St Matthew*), but they are not likely to 'remain in the dark' about other, more familiar resonances the characters employ, even when they do so with a not always easy aplomb: Cain and Abel, Golgotha and the rumour that Christ went barefoot. Lines like 'Do you think God sees me?' and 'Christ have mercy on us' introduce additional imperatives, as does the Boy's report that Godot sports a patriarchal white beard.

The tree itself – of knowledge? of life? – encourages further rumination. Judas, to name one, made quick use of it, as did St Sebastian's tormentors, who tied the young Roman soldier-martyr to a tree and shot him with arrows (according to Tom Stoppard, he died of fright).[8] Beckett's tramps dither too long about weights and belts and measures and other 'whereas-es' (the tree fails, too, as a hiding place, and it's even more pathetic as a position in yoga). It may be a willow – 'No more weeping' – but that attribution, too, is disturbingly noncommittal. No wonder the critic Hugh Kenner referred to such a hefty biblical texture as 'checks that will bounce'. 'Christianity is a mythology with which I am perfectly familiar,' the playwright demurred. 'So naturally I use it.'[9] And in that lofty tradition, configured as it is with first and second comings (and goings) in a world without end, *waiting* serves as the ultimate mythos indeed.

The play's many literary allusions are similarly compromised, conspiratorial and everywhere unyielding: Hamlet's 'Words, words' and the string of mock-quotations lifted so effortlessly from (among other sources) Shelley, Dante, Hölderlin, Calderón, Dickens, Schopenhauer, Verlaine, Bishop Berkeley and Joyce. When one critic complained that Beckett made his characters sound as though they had PhDs, his response was very much to the point: who's to say that they hadn't?[10] Here the author shows his hand at being both eclectic and pan-European; and his training as a prizewinning student of modern languages at Trinity College, Dublin pays off, although not necessarily in terms that help his reader or offer any easy access to the play in performance. ('A very fair scholar I was too,' Beckett wrote elsewhere. 'No thought, but a great memory.')[11] A rarefied game of blind-man's-bluff, *Godot*'s intertextuality, however, never interferes with the play's dramatic action – if the audience gets the reference, that's fine; if not, not – though what the playwright once disparaged as 'the loutishness of learning' will haunt him for the rest of his writing life.[12]

How, then, do we enter the richly simulated stage world of *Waiting for Godot*?

The play is, first and foremost, a work of its time written for its time. *Godot*'s defoliated landscape, so familiar to us and so full of suggestion, carries the burden of something perhaps more horrific than an existential void. Beckett composed *Godot* in the ugly aftermath of the Second World War, when much of Europe and Asia was left behind as an empty, 'ruinstrewn' land. Set against the devastation of Auschwitz and Nagasaki, the minimalist set for Beckett's play can appear as both symbolic and emblematic, at other times even grotesquely carnivalesque. Historical perspective therefore richly informs the meaning of the play, though it does not for one moment overwhelm it.

Beckett's actions during the Second World War, it should be noted, greatly expand the template for historicising this play.[13] A citizen of neutral Ireland, he could stay with impunity in occupied Paris, his adopted home, even after the city fell under German occupation. But when the SS and their willing French collaborators began the systematic harassment of many of his friends, including the round-up of those who were Jewish, he could no longer 'stand with [his] arms folded'.[14] He did a lot more than that, joining an underground cell and translating stolen documents dealing with the movement of German troops before they could be smuggled to

Allied headquarters in London. Under torture, two members of his Resistance group named names, and Beckett was soon on the run. He took shelter in a number of safe houses before a *passeur* helped him find his way into hiding in the south of France. And it was there in the Vaucluse, cut off for the first time from his family in Ireland and under the threat of imminent denunciation, sitting out the war but ever mindful of his 'Boy Scout stuff',[15] that the playwright could experience at first hand what *waiting* was all about:

Was I sleeping, while the others suffered? Am I sleeping
now? Tomorrow, when I wake, or think I do, what shall
I say of today? That with Estragon my friend, at this place,
until the fall of night, I waited for Godot? That Pozzo
passed, with his carrier, and that he spoke to us? Probably.
But in all that what truth will there be? . . . Astride of a
grave and a difficult birth, the gravedigger puts on the
forceps. We have time to grow old. The air is full of our
cries. (*He listens.*) But habit is a great deadener . . . At me
too someone is looking, of me too someone is saying, He
is sleeping, he knows nothing, let him sleep on. (*Pause.*)
I can't go on! (*Pause.*) What have I said?

Vladimir's climactic speech, summarising and encapsulating the play's rising action, deftly marks its historical framework with profound metaphysical inclinations.

And it is precisely this appealing duality that Alan Schneider had in mind in his observation, already cited, that *Godot* was 'no longer merely a play. It has become a condition of life.'[16]

Such a precarious state of mind has invited from the play's first appearance a busy field of philosophical commentary and, more recently, critical theory. It has always been difficult to resist the temptation to do so, this despite the playwright's insistence that

'I am not a philosopher.' Very much the work of 'a fifties writer', Beckett's *Waiting for Godot* as a piece for performance easily represents and perhaps even clarifies a world in which existence precedes essence; and it does so far more accessibly and with much greater immediacy than the great study undertaken by his contemporary Jean-Paul Sartre, *Being and Nothingness*.[17] Martin Esslin, among Beckett's first responders, understood, moreover, that *Godot* was securely anchored in the reality of its genre, upon which it signalled a profound variation in style, subject and sensibility. The play helped to change the perception of what could be brought into the arena of stage representation. When he coined the term 'the theatre of the absurd', setting Beckett alongside such fellow practitioners as Ionesco, Adamov, Pinter and later Albee, Esslin reminded us that the contingencies of playwriting demanded to be considered practically before they might be rendered as metaphysical[18] – how to get from *here*, so to speak, to *there*.

It is naturally in the theatre, then, that *Godot* reaches for and ultimately achieves its ideal supremacy. Roles for actors here can be challenging, and they will sometimes require an ecstatically mannered interpretation, for Beckett uses every old trouper trick in the trade. Vaudeville, *commedia dell'arte*, music-hall routines and choreographic schtick borrowed with hopeless abandon from the silent movies of the 1920s and 30s will be used liberally and dynamically. The sometimes absurd episodes and pointless repetition involving hat tricks, a monologue that gets out of control, pathetic dance steps, a song shaped as a round poem, metatheatrical exits when a bladder is about to burst, spontaneous kicks in the shin, speaking while chewing a carrot, a discourse on the ownership of discarded chicken bones, falling asleep mid-scene and farting while four characters lie prone on the open road may initially appear disconnected, and yet their purposefulness is always unified by pace, rigour and ambience. Indeed, the play establishes its steady momentum through a careful orchestration of such a bizarre series of little 'canters'. 'Come on, Gogo,' Didi reminds his reluctant acting partner who deliberately misses his cues. 'Return the ball, can't you, once in a way.'

The plot is minuscule, easy to summarise, but there's just enough of it to keep the repertory of tricks going while two down-at-heels keep their appointment, twice, waiting for someone less scrupulous than they are, the shadowy figure who won't come on 'Board'. Why do they do so, and why does Godot continue to skip out on them? The Boy's answer at the end of each act is more puzzling than revelatory: 'I don't know, Sir,' the same response the wounded author himself got when he asked a mentally disturbed man why he plunged a knife into his chest on the Coeur-de-Vey, a small dead-end street off the avenue d'Orléans, now the avenue Général-Leclerc.[19] Pants fall down; but for the play's imminent closure they must be pulled back 'ON' (it's 'Never neglect the little things in life' all over again). The drama ends with the frozen picture of two moonlit men holding hands, reciting exit lines they will never put into action:

Vladimir Well, shall we go?
Estragon Yes, let's go.

And it is finally this image, as it fades, that remains lodged for ever in the audience's imagination.

Going and not going, now, soon or later – not going places, really – has always been one of *Godot*'s memorable refrains:

Estragon Let's go.
Vladimir We can't.
Estragon Why not?
Vladimir We're waiting for Godot.

Rooted in a rhythm of return, Estragon's delinquent 'Ah!' highlights the work's architectural frame, which can be alternately –

and sometimes simultaneously – endearing and murderously frustrating in its simplicity. 'All true grace is economical,' the playwright told the English director Peter Hall.[20] And yet the play's long history in production shows just how generous this text's economy can be in providing collaborative opportunities for Beckett's many interpreters in performance – and that list includes designers and directors as well as actors in the international community of theatre practitioners. Such latitude was very much in evidence in Roger Blin's initial production of *En attendant Godot* in 1953.[21] Beckett was impressed with the young director's discipline and discretion when he saw his modest staging of *The Ghost Sonata*, 'true to the letter and the spirit' of Strindberg's ambitious chamber play. Blin, for his part, said he was attracted to *Godot* not because of its multi-dimensionality, which completely eluded him at the time, but because it was inexpensive to produce. His Left Bank company was always short of funds, and he knew he could count on financial support from the cultural ministry by mounting a new work written in French by a non-native speaker. Besides, the other Beckett play on offer, *Eleutheria* (the Greek word for freedom), required multiple sets and a cast of sixteen, excluding itself from serious consideration. With Pierre Latour as Estragon, Lucien Raimbourg as Vladimir and Jean Martin as Lucky, Blin himself took on the role of Pozzo in his own production. Sergio Gerstein's decor for the small proscenium stage was straightforward and uncluttered, and formal attire past its prime, including bowler hats, was borrowed and dusted off from the closets of family and friends. Turnips and carrots were easy to come by in the outdoor markets nearby.

Strange as it may seem today, the script of *En attendant Godot* was turned down by every established production team to whom it had been offered. Suzanne Dumesnil, the playwright's lifelong companion (she later became his wife), urged Beckett to make the connection with Blin after seeing his faithful rendering of Strindberg. She was also trying to help get Beckett's prose fiction published at the same time, but with a similar lack of success. The only agent who took her up on this was Jérôme Lindon, whose Éditions de Minuit had recently purchased the old equipment from an underground press. In 1952 he also published a pre-production version of the play. So profound was the impact of *Godot* once it achieved performance, however – the playwright Jean Anouilh compared the importance of the opening night to the premiere in Paris of Pirandello's *Six Characters in Search of an Author* some fifty years earlier – that almost everyone who was in and out of the city that season claimed to have seen it. Elmar Tophoven, a graduate student from Germany, did; he translated the play into his own language, and by the fall of the same year his *Warten auf Godot* was staged at the Berlin Theatre Festival, only a few months after Blin's French production toured the country.

Beckett's translation of the play into English was ready for production two years later. His choice of composing *Godot* in French, then working as self-translator, must be considered as something much more than a curiosity, however. After returning to liberated Paris in 1945 and finding his apartment on the rue des Favorites remarkably intact, he made a deliberate leap into French for his new writing. While waiting for the war to end in Free France, *en attendant* so to speak, he completed his novel *Watt*, still slogging away in English. But there was 'something' about the literary use of his first language that he was beginning to distrust, a kind of 'lack of brakes'. It was easier to write in French 'sans style'.[22] He was of course referring to his grand scheme for the trilogy of novels we know from his translations as *Molloy*, *Malone Dies* and *The Unnamable*. *Godot* was composed in what he described as an 'interval' between the first two, shifting his genre but not his adopted linguistic métier. Besides, Beckett was beginning to sound, ironically, increasingly more Irish in French than he ever did in English, as though he were approaching his text twice-removed.

Setting the two *Godot*s side by side, as they are arranged and printed in the bilingual edition published by Grove Press in 2006 (Beckett's centenary year), allows us to see how each version offers a commentary and a gloss on the other. In French, for example, Didi reminds his recalcitrant sidekick that they went grape-harvesting together for a man named Bonnelly in the Mâcon country; in English Didi can no longer 'think of the name of the man' or even remember 'the name of the place'. Gogo repudiates such misguided nostalgia in both languages, insisting that he has 'puked his puke of a life away' here, in the very same place, in 'the Cackon country', relying as he does on a geographical neologism more pointedly ridiculous in French than in English. Sometimes the effect works the other way around, especially for an Irishman, as when the poet-manqué Gogo makes fun of how pretentious Anglo-Saxons can be when they mouth the word *calm*: 'Calm . . . calm. . . (*Dreamily.*) The English say cawm.' (That's funny for the French, too, but in an entirely different way, for their *calme* is hard to pronounce).

Details like these steadily accumulate. Yet unlike the translations Beckett undertook of his other plays – French to English and, later, English to French – they do little to alter the fundamental mood and atmosphere of the play, which remains fairly consistent in both versions. One scene plays very differently in each language nonetheless, and that is Lucky's speech. In English his extended monologue can become progressively maddening and alarming – 'quaquaquaqua' – if not downright frightening, while on the French stage it plays itself out as an elaborate and hilarious parody of the well-worn *philosophe* tradition, Descartes to Derrida. Other contrasts are the result of inherent linguistic differences, and a writer such as Beckett can be relied upon to put them to quick use: French can be by its very nature a more playful language for the belletrist, whereas English, steady as it goes, is always in love with the practical and the concrete. And to complicate matters, there is in the case of *Waiting for Godot*, as is in most of Beckett's writing in English, the distinct sound of an Irish inflection, which Beckett spoke with an upper-class Dublin accent – another culture and another idiolect altogether.

Several of these contrasts were very much on display when *Godot* was first presented in the author's skilful translation on both sides of the Atlantic.[23] Peter Hall directed the English-language premiere of the play in London at the Arts Theatre Club, where audiences gave it a chilly reception until two major critics, Harold Hobson and Kenneth Tynan, recognised its powerful dramatic pull. 'It is exasperating. It is insidiously exciting,' wrote Hobson prophetically in the *Sunday Times*. He urged his readers to see Beckett's new play because they would discover there 'something that will securely lodge in a corner of your mind for as long as you live'. In *The Observer* Tynan coined a new word, proud to count himself the first 'godotista'. Beckett, who saw Hall's London production five times, disliked almost everything about it, however; the stage was too busy, the narrative too slow, the statements too meaningful and the comedy too broad. 'It's ahl wrahng!' he told Alan Schneider, who was soon to run into even greater difficulties when he brought the play to America in 1956.

The story of Schneider and his initial encounter with *Waiting for Godot* is now legendary.[24] The play opened at the Coconut Grove Playhouse in Miami, where it was billed, inappropriately, as 'the laugh sensation of two continents'. Bert Lahr, who starred as Estragon, probably got things right when he said that performing *Godot* in Miami was 'like doing *Giselle* in Roseland'. The audience walked out in droves. The production, nonetheless, moved on to New York, this time with Herbert Berghof as replacement director. In order to increase interest in the work as well as prolong its run, a discussion with the audience was held after each performance, the first time such an event was scheduled on Broadway. Walter Kerr lived to regret his nasty review of *Godot* as an 'intellectual fruit-bowl', though in terms of ticket sales his philistinism had already done considerable damage, from which the show never recovered. Yet even in this well-intentioned New York production, the tone became overly emphatic, and the play never found its audience. The situation did not improve when Schneider returned to *Godot* in 1961 for its television adaptation on 'Play of the Week'; each time Zero Mostel as Gogo uttered 'Ah!' his exclamation was punctuated by the intrusive reverberations of an echo chamber, rendering everything ponderous if not downright dull.

The potential fault lines in bringing *Waiting for Godot* to the stage were therefore already exposed in the work's initial productions in Paris, London, Miami and New York. For the obvious challenge in bringing this play to life has always been how *not* to make things boring while remaining true to the play, not to confuse the representation of nothingness with the void that is nothing itself.[25] This is a 'tragicomedy' after all, though productions of *Godot* risk limiting its scope by pulling it in one direction or the other. The text, however, is a model of dramatic balance and proportion as it moves its characters very deliberately from one routine to the next. That same self-sufficiency is apparent even in the opening moment, when Gogo puts into play the first incantation of his memorable line, 'Nothing to be done.' Sitting on a low mound, he is of course struggling to remove a boot, which he fails to do. Didi, for his part, hears things quite differently:

> I'm beginning to come round to that opinion. All my life
> I've tried to put it from me, saying, Vladimir, be reasonable,
> you haven't yet tried everything. And I resumed the struggle.
> (*He broods, musing on the struggle.*)

So much is packed into this simple exchange, and it happens so quickly – it can even be the first of many laugh lines – that we can easily miss how efficiently the metaphysical has been embedded in the seemingly pathetic. There's a lot more of this sort of thing to come, for the play is constructed as a string of semi-autonomous routines designed to amplify the initial orchestration; and they do so even when the pieces don't neatly mesh, are hard to interpret and may leave us perplexed. *Godot* keeps meaning on the move, to hide it, change it, undermine it, multiply it. If the meanings and moods feel elusive, well, they are; an explanation would be an intrusion. *Godot* 'flows and eddies and twists and turns and stops and sweeps', observed Ronald Pickup, who played Lucky in London in 2009.[26] Beckett gives his tramps 'exercises', 'movements', 'elevations', 'relaxations' and 'elongations' to perform; there's much to do while waiting for Godot, and even more to ponder. The two principal characters are even allowed to 'abuse' one another, though their strategy in this respect remains strictly (though stingingly) verbal:

> **Vladimir** Ceremonious ape!
> **Estragon** Punctilious pig! . . .
> **Vladimir** Moron!
> **Estragon** That's the idea, let's abuse each other . . .
> **Vladimir** Moron!
> **Estragon** Vermin!
> **Vladimir** Abortion!
> **Estragon** Morpion!
> **Vladimir** Sewer-rat!
> **Estragon** Curate!
> **Vladimir** Cretin!
> **Estragon** (*with finality*) Crritic!

This particular 'canter' has come to an end with a flag-waving *mot juste*; the characters pause, perhaps are even granted a moment to reflect on the success or failure of their pitter-patter – but stasis and immobility is to be avoided at all costs, as is the silence which has its own way of intruding its presence. In such non-verbal moments the signs of intimacy are unambiguously piled up, offering actors the opportunity to convey complicated emotional signals marked by a series of sometimes obvious, sometimes obscure inflection points. The effect of severance can be startling, but bracingly intimate, too, as the vanishing act that is stage (and human) experience stands still and whispers dark mysteries to us. And then Didi and Gogo doggedly resume, swiftly moving on so as not to forget their lines for the next motif.

The really big routine here is Pozzo and Lucky, such a command performance in the first act that Beckett can't resist the opportunity to work a dramatic variation on it in the second. There's suddenly a great deal happening on this stage, when all is *said* and *done*. Send in the clowns: Beckett does this, too. The alternation of moods is extraordinary; moments of cruelty and indifference alternate with other moments of extreme tenderness. And these differences, while significant, do not necessarily change the overall effect and atmosphere of the play; in fact, they support and sustain it. 'Pozzo and Lucky' is a skit so rich in theatricality and dramatic potential that Didi and Gogo even consider 'playing' it themselves, as contrasted figures seem to be all the rage. This is, then, a self-proclaimed tragicomedy stripped for everything *but* inaction.[27] Yet the final, cruellest routine of all is still to come, and Didi serves as the world-weary narrator whose job it is to proclaim it as such: 'Off we go again.' Each act concludes with the entry of a hesitant young Boy, who announces, not altogether unexpectedly, that Mr Godot will not come today. 'We have to come back tomorrow.'

It is not surprising, then, that Beckett's simple eloquence in the structure of this play should have earned *Waiting for Godot* such a wide international appeal. Specific to the stage, but widely applicable in its resonances, the story could take place anywhere, which, if not exactly the same thing as saying it could take place everywhere, comes pretty close: '*A country road. A tree. Evening.*' Tom Stoppard, whose curtain line in *Jumpers* pays stunning tribute to *Waiting for Godot* ('Wham, bam, thank you, Sam'), noted that Beckett's play 'doesn't need to gain strength from its own time and place; it has its own strength . . . The play is a universal metaphor precisely because it wasn't designed as being a metaphor for anything in particular. The true subject matter of *Waiting for Godot* is that it's about two tramps waiting for somebody.'[28] Only stage time and stage place tie it down.

Waiting for Godot is therefore the play that makes the case for a truly borderless Beckett. Working from the playwright's French and English versions, translators quickly made the script available in a wide variety of European languages.[29] The play was even produced in sometimes unusual and unfamiliar places, including an Argentine working-man's theatre in a dusty mountainous town near the Chilean frontier. One exception to such widespread accessibility was the ban imposed by the Soviet Union and several of its satellite states, where *Godot* was condemned as a prime example of western decadence and despair. Bertolt Brecht, nevertheless, appreciated the work's open performative potential, despite his commitment to the sometimes one-dimensionality of communist causality. He read the play for its harrowing political overtones, where Lucky is the ill-treated proletarian under the thumb of a merciless capitalist boss. His student, Peter Palitsch, later produced the play in the former Yugoslavia with a Brechtian overlay in sharp relief.

Such an approach is not necessarily unauthorised in the text, even though the heavy-handedness in this instance severely limits its possibilities: to an Irish audience, for example, the self-important Pozzo might be easily recognisable as the big-house Protestant from 'the manor' who wields a more than metaphorical whip. Because of official censorship and a general uneasiness with western theatre, the Arab states have been largely unwelcoming to *Waiting for Godot*; and Beckett himself refused to give permission for his plays to be performed in South Africa under the apartheid regime. He made one exception: an all-black production at the Market Theatre, Cape Town, in 1976, following the Soweto riots, allowing the accents to fall where they may. As of this writing, Chinese audiences are only just beginning their encounter with *Godot*; a full-scale production of the play did not reach Shanghai until 2009.

In the United States Herbert Blau looked at hopeless inequality through the lens of incarceration when he took his San Francisco Actor's Workshop production to the maximum security prison at San Quentin: if there ever was an audience who understood the life sentence of waiting, this was it. The Swedish director Jan Jonson took this relationship one step further by casting inmates from the jail at Kumla in the major roles; when he took the show on the road, however, his actor-convicts made a run for it. 'Perhaps they had no time to wait,' the playwright told the director when he heard about this outcome. Inspired rather than dismayed, Jonson repeated his work on *Godot* with another set of more reliable performers, now drawn from lifers at San Quentin itself. Blau's celebrated work on *Waiting for Godot*, as is well known, led to the founding of the San Quentin Drama Workshop, and a pardon for Rick Cluchey, who became the company's artistic director and principal actor. Beckett remained one of the group's most faithful supporters, sometimes serving as an adviser to Cluchey's productions of his own plays.

That *Godot* can successfully sustain any number of impositions, even migrations, is a lasting tribute to its status as a modern-day classic. In Japan, where Beckett's work has a wide following, the play has been staged in both Noh and Kabuki style; and in Israel, where the author of *Godot* is often called 'the ultimate Jewish writer' despite his severe Protestant upbringing, the play has received at least one volatile reading. In the Haifa Municipal Theatre's highly controversial production, Lucky was cast as a subservient Israeli Arab under the yoke of an imperial and insensitive master. Distinctive Hebrew accents established marginalisation, hierarchy and characterisation all at once. Susan Sontag worked another turn of the screw into the work's foundation when, in the midst of war and genocide, she 'reinvented' the play in the 1993 project she called *Waiting for Godot in Sarajevo*. ('The tickets are free,' Erika Munk observed. 'Everything else comes at great cost.')[30] *Godot*'s meaning was similarly localised by the artist and activist Paul Chan when he worked with the Classical Theater of Harlem's outdoor production in New Orleans in 2007. His Creative Team presented the play on various street corners in still-destroyed neighbourhoods in Ward 9 after the failure of the Bush Administration to deal with the tragedy of Hurricane Katrina.

Beckett was generally unhappy with productions of *Godot* that departed from the specifics of the sturdy *mise-en-scène* he imagined for the play in 1949, although he was considerably more generous with himself when working on liberal revisions of the text for the Berlin Schiller-Werkstatt Theater in 1975, which he directed himself (his emendations can be carefully tracked and traced in the first volume of *The Theatrical Notebooks of Samuel Beckett*).[31] The playwright was always opposed, for example, to the concept of staging *Godot* as a play about women, since, as he said, 'women don't have prostates' (in 1991 Bruno Boussagol nonetheless directed a rare all-female version at the Avignon Festival). Since Beckett's death in 1989, his Estate has become even more hardlined, not always to the play's advantage. Yet despite such strictures, theatre practitioners continue to bring enormous vitality and originality to their vision of this play, mostly by paying careful attention to its clean lines as a vehicle for performance.

Mike Nichols performed an important service to the work, reminding us of its essentially comic texture after too many years of reverence and gravitas (always a show's death knell). Steve Martin and Robin Williams were cast in the principal roles for his 1988 production at Lincoln Center. Bill Irwin as Lucky, a restrained and recalcitrant mime who seemed to measure every two-step shuffle, was a perfect antidote to their broadly played aerobics. That same year Louis le Brocquy designed an evocative and atmospheric set for the highly lyrical *Godot* performed at the Gate Theatre in Dublin, where Barry McGovern and Tom Hickey portrayed Didi and Gogo as the Irish itinerants they always were. And the year 2009 saw two popular renditions of the work by master actors on both sides of the Atlantic: vaudeville was much in the air for Patrick Stewart and Ian McKellen at the Haymarket Theatre in London, while in New York Bill Irwin was a thoughtful, cautious and sensitive Didi to Nathan Lane's runaway Gogo. Pozzos loomed large: John Goodman's girth virtually monumental on Broadway, Simon Callow fussy, even at times prissy in the West End (the semiotics of sitting down took on a whole new meaning in his palpable display). Both productions highlighted something fundamental about the art and craft so central to the impact of *Waiting for Godot*: metaphysics notwithstanding, Beckett has written some really great roles for actors; and those parts and the lines written for them have had from the start a tendency to outsize the play for which they were written: 'Nothing to be done.'

But it's not true that in this drama 'nobody comes' and 'nobody goes'. Pozzo and Lucky and even the young Boy do so, twice, full of mystery, menace and a surprising allure for a work that 'is striving all the time to avoid definition'.[32] And at those highly dramatic moments when *Godot* presents us with a backward glance – 'Pity we haven't got a bit of rope' – it is commenting on itself and on the human condition at one and the same time. Does that make it sound pretentious? 'Crritic[s]' beware.

Just where do Didi and Gogo – and we with them – 'come in here' and, more to the point, where do we go from here? What the play offers us is a 'reasonable percentage' by way of its own con-clusion, a directive that is anything but tentative: 'ON!'

When the National Theatre in London asked playwrights, direc-tors, actors and journalists to list the ten plays of the twentieth century that they considered most 'significant', *Waiting for Godot* came in first.

CHAPTER 2

From Dada to Didi: Beckett and the Art of His Century

In *Lessness*, a short and enigmatic prose piece originally published on a single page of *The New Statesman* on 1 May 1970, Beckett abandoned his rigorous and unusually fastidious method of composition. In marked contrast to the procedures he followed in nearly all of his mature work, where a term like over-determined can seem like an understatement, this time he went slumming: he wrote sixty sentences on separate pieces of paper, threw them into a box, then took them out one at a time. *Lessness* displays them in the order in which they emerged. He repeated the process a second time, letting chance have its persuasive say, so that each sentence appears only twice, both times in a different sequence.

Written initially as French *Sans* before Beckett completed his own translation into 'strange English', the piece has an obvious and even more fundamental French patrimony:

Take a newspaper.
Take a pair of scissors.
Choose an article as long as you are planning to make your poem.
Cut out the article.
Then cut out each of the words that make up this article and put them in a bag.
Shake it gently.
Then take out the scraps one after another in the order in which they left the bag.

Copy conscientiously.
The poem will be like you.
And here you are a writer, infinitely original and endowed
with a sensibility that is charming though beyond the
understanding of the vulgar.[1]

Tristan Tzara's famous manifesto on 'How to Make a Dadaist Poem' is, however, full of marvellous inconsistencies. It's hard to believe, for example, that the artist Hans (also known as Jean) Arp, who adapted this technique for his own purposes, wouldn't have been tempted to upset such accidental arrangements when he tore paper into squares of various sizes, then dropped them onto a sheet of paper and pasted them into place where they fell. He did the same with his abstract wood reliefs, generating forms from automatic drawings which he then had a carpenter cut into shapes. Did Arp ever shift them a bit, or choose some pieces of paper rather than others, because they looked better that way?

Such questionable 'readymades' are perhaps even more likely to become readymades-assisted when we turn our attention to what Kurt Schwitters termed the basic 'elements of poetry' – 'letters, syllables, words' and 'sentences'.[2] Beckett's modulated images seem to have arrived from some other world, as if the author were telling us that he planned to keep his options open, to make a sweeping formal investigation of representation without declaring his absolute faith in it. It is of course here that Beckett plays his hand – and, sophisticated writer that he is, he can be counted on to play it well. The final sentence of *Lessness*, for example, is poised as follows: 'Figment dawn dispeller of figments and the other called dusk.' While it is not mathematically impossible for such lexical and phonetic elements to cohere – every hand dealt in a game of cards is, by fiat, equally improbable – in the case of *Lessness* sentence 120, the remarkable and final one, concludes on the hard sound of . . . *k* . . . and 'dusk' is, well, dusk.[3]

Lessness is full of other Dada headaches. As Beckett told Martin Esslin when he was preparing a reading of the piece for broadcast on BBC Radio in February 1971, 'It is composed of six statement groups each containing ten sentences, i.e. sixty sentences in all.' Each order is assigned a different paragraph structure, the whole arranged 'in 2 × 12 = 24 paragraphs'; and Beckett further pointed out that each statement group is 'formally differentiated' so that the ten sentences composing it are 'signed' by 'certain elements common to all':

Group A – Collapse of refuge – Sign: 'true refuge'.

Group B – Outer world – Sign: 'earth-sky' juxtaposed or apart.

Group C – body exposed – Sign: 'little body'.

Group D – Refuge forgotten – Sign: 'all gone from mind'.

Group E – Past and future denied – Sign: 'never' – except in the one sentence 'figment dawn etc'.

Group F – Past and future affirmed – Sign: future tense.[4]

So much for the free gestures of chance; and so much for taking letters, words, syllables and sentences haphazardly out of a hat. This is therefore something more, and quite different indeed, from what Stéphane Mallarmé had in mind when he scattered his words across the page in the poem 'Un Coup de Dés' ('A Throw of the Dice') in 1897.

Beckett will be similarly circumspect in his borrowings from other Dada strategies, and no more so than in *Not I*. That play has become so well known among Beckett specialists, and indeed within the international theatre community as a whole, that it is perhaps difficult to recapture its stunning impact on audiences who saw the 1972 premiere performances at Lincoln Center in New York and, a few months later, at the Royal Court Theatre in London. The television adaptation for the BBC, featuring a bravura performance by Billie Whitelaw as Mouth, made it, if anything, even more notorious. Here was a play, as the author himself wryly noted about its companion piece, *That Time*, which could only be explained as 'something out of Beckett'.[5] But perhaps not quite. Tzara's dramatis personae in *The Gas Heart* (1920) include not only Mouth, but also Eye, Ear, Nose, Neck and Eyebrow as well. And another work from the same Dada delirium, *Humulus the Mute* (1929), a romp in four scenes by Jean Anouilh and Jean Aurenche, makes use of a similar Mouth–Auditor dualism to structure 'a bitterly silly, pointless joke, in the purist Dadaist tradition'.[6] Yet neither work, ambitious as it is, displays the same careful attention to scenographic detail characteristic of the technical demands of *Not I*, where the design elements of lighting and luminosity are so essential to Beckett's allure that they become not only idiosyncratic but almost iconographic in the plays that follow, and where passages of volumetric shading suggest a concealed third dimension.

Destabilising, insidious and thrilling, visuals in Beckett are always an important part of the theatrical mix. If the first audiences for *Not I* were stymied in their attempt to locate a precedent for the image advanced on stage with so much precision and authority, they were nonetheless likely to find this in the unlimited formal and expressive liberties taken by legendary avant-gardists. The subversive tactics of groups such as the Cabaret Voltaire in Zurich were swiftly taken up by other practitioners in Berlin, Hanover, Cologne, Paris and eventually New York. Making it *really* new, and often less concerned to enlighten than to outrage the public and create a scandal, artists including Max Ernst, Hugo Ball, Marcel Duchamp, Man Ray, Sophie Trauber, Giorgio de Chirico and most especially René Magritte, arranged their materials in a sensational variety of improbable contexts. Eyes materialise with uncanny regularity, and in unexpected places. Everywhere one feels the sense of what the French call, quite accurately, *dépaysement*. Setting perspective askew, vision itself is called into question.

A museum survey of Dada curated in 2006, which originated at the Pompidou Centre in Paris before travelling to the National Gallery in Washington, D.C. and eventually to the Museum of Modern Art in New York, made this abundantly clear: 450 works by fifty artists highlighted both the range and proliferation of styles that are both mutually supportive and exclusive.[7] 'Dada, Dada, Dada,' Tzara wrote with considerable brio, was synonymous with 'Freedom', embracing as it did 'a roaring of tense colours,' an 'interlacing of opposites and of all contradictions, grotesques' and 'inconsistencies'. In a word, Dada, taking conventions apart and exposing their artifice, was 'LIFE'.[8]

What saved Dada from oblivion was its playful sense of the absurd, its healthy dose of scepticism, and a bag of tricks designed to *épater les bourgeois*. Beckett displays these sensibilities in *Breath*, where his random detritus anticipates the raw energy of punk graphics, and also in *Quad*, where the celebration of colour, followed by its lack, traces the rhythmic footsteps of a Dada journey to nowhere *in particular* – and back again, '100,000 years later'.[9] In other places Beckett can also transform bruitism, the habit of making noise for no sake other than itself, into his own 'matter of fundamental sounds' – and in this case the 'joke' is very much 'intended'.[10] Uncontrollable flatulence, a Dada speciality (in 1928 Antonin Artaud was fascinated by this problem in Vitrac's *Victor: ou les enfants au pouvoir*), is experienced by more than one Beckett hero. 'Who farted?' enquires a wearier-than-weary Vladimir, lying prone on the stage with three fellow acolytes. Molloy, a journeyman with a passion for precision, even calculates his by their frequency and number. Fortunately in this case Beckett spares his reader the obsessive systematisation of confusion involved in scoring, for example, the croaking of three frogs in an earlier novel, *Watt*:

Krak! — — — — — — — —
Krek! — — — — Krek! — —
Krik! — — Krik! — — Krik! —

Krak! — — — — — — — —
— — Krek! — — — — Krek!
— Krik! — — Krik! — — Krik!

I can't – and I won't – go on.

Beckett's biographer James Knowlson reminds us that the *drame bourgeois* the author wrote while still a student at Trinity College, Dublin, called *Le Kid*, a parody of Corneille and Charlot (Charlie Chaplin), participates in the same heady rapture of irreverence and iconoclasm; the playwright even remembered writing it in the 'by then somewhat jaded' spirit of some of the early experiments of Dada.[11] And as late as the 'close of a long day' in *Rockaby* (1981), one of Beckett's most memorable female figures is discovered alone on stage in a rocking chair, still 'Fuck[ing]' around with] what Tzara called 'life'.

Beckett's works can also be referenced, albeit somewhat more obliquely, with certain spectacular moments in the surrealist tradition, Dada's far more accomplished stepchild. Winnie planted in her mound of earth in *Happy Days* is a not altogether obscure allusion to the unwelcome figures similarly buried in the final frames of *Un Chien andalou*; and Molloy's talk traverses the same terrain when the character's visual attention is momentarily arrested in the novel's early pages by the haunting image of a dead donkey's eye. The close-up which announces Beckett's 22-minute 'comic and unreal' *Film* is similarly bound to Buñuel as much as it is to Bishop Berkeley ('To be is to be perceived'). Even more tantalising is the fact that the filmscript appeared in the same special surrealist number of *This Quarter* (September 1932) in which Beckett's translations of poems by René Crevel, Paul Éluard and André Breton can be found.

Critics, myself included, have not always been entirely certain about what to do in the face of so many 'demented particulars'. On the one hand, this has resulted in a dazzling series of studies suggestively linking Beckett to the art of his century ('Beckett and —' whatever the blank may be); on the other, it sometimes emboldens 'dons on overdrive' (see Tom Stoppard's *Arcadia*) to construct a complete theory of aesthetics based on such waning literary evidence.[12] *No try no fail.* But what led the playwright from Dada to Didi may very well point us in another direction entirely, one that has far more to do with inspiration than influence. Beckett found in Dada, even after it had morphed into surrealism, a climate of spontaneity that offered him a new vocabulary for fracture and ruptured certainties. What it did not offer him was a formal structure to meet its own demands; and this was the domain Beckett would make so securely his own. In a certain sense, in works like *Lessness* and *Not I*, as elsewhere, he took Dada at its own word; and then he took it one step further.

That Beckett was a formalist is hardly what anyone by this date would call big news. Even his first commentators were thrilled to seize upon the early interview in which he held forth – a rarity for him – on the virtues of finding 'a form to accommodate the mess'.[13] The Dada adventurists and their rearguard associates who preceded him on the Left Bank – the movement was on its last legs by the time Beckett arrived in Paris in the late 1920s – may have called for the abolition of 'the old style', as well as a much-needed end to 'salon' art with a capital A, but they were not necessarily successful or even interested in finding a 'shape that matters'.[14] Beckett was.

And that would make all the difference. Both by inclination and training, Beckett was fascinated by artists with a strict and highly disciplined sense of decorum: Dante, of course, whose *terza rima* was a model of symmetry and lyrical concision; Joyce, the 'synthesiser' who sought to incorporate nothing less than the entire history of western civilisation into the sixteen-year project first known as *Work in Progress*, then *Finnegans Wake*; and, to a lesser extent, Proust, another writer's writer whose elegant Latinate sentences have the potential to unlock the 'last fancies' and painful mysteries of an entire lost world. Beckett was also well-trained in the classics, 'a part' of which always remained sacred to him; as the intrepid Winnie observes:

One loses one's classics. (*Pause.*) Oh not all. (*Pause*). A part. (*Pause.*) A part remains. (*Pause.*) That is what I find so wonderful, a part remains, of one's classics, to help one through the day. (*Pause.*) Oh yes, many mercies, many mercies.

In the visual arts, too, Beckett was drawn to the precision of a Caravaggio, with his seamless control over light on canvas when less did not seem possible; and in music his taste ran to the evocative power in the structured measures and 'rigid economy' of the late Schubert and Beethoven, not to the eccentricities and rodomontades of the mostly Mozartian variety. Lyric opera – over the top – was strictly out of the question.[15]

This brief discussion hinges on one final issue, and one that goes to the heart of the matter concerning Beckett and the art of his century. Like any major figure, Beckett is both representative of his moment in time and someone who stands apart from it; and that is what brings additional resonance to the durability of the writing. This chapter focuses on Beckett's debt to Dada, but it might just as well have been centred on any number of groundbreaking movements in twentieth-century European art. In Beckett's work we can sense any *and* all of these powerful forces at play, although not one of them on its own can fully certify his achievement or explain it 'all strange away'. 'The classifiers are the obscurantists,' he wrote to Mary Manning Howe from Berlin in

1936. Despite reports to the contrary (rather dated now), this very particular author is no deader than any of his texts; and despite our attempts to track these down through the multiple associations and cross-references they give rise to, they constantly elude us. 'What tenderness in these little words, what savagery' – that is what keeps his readers going, 'call that going, call that on', fellow travellers all. The same might be said (and in fact has been said) of artists from earlier periods, Michelangelo certainly, but Shakespeare and Titian as well. In my own generation of critics it has become neither fashionable nor politically correct to make such claims for exceptionalism, although it's surely no longer possible to use with any credibility a phrase that begins with 'Writers like Beckett . . .'. In the twentieth century there simply aren't any. For in his 'case nought' the forms are 'many' indeed, *mirabile dictu*, 'in which the unchanging seeks release from' – what? – 'its form [*Lessness*]'.

CHAPTER 3

Beckett's Landscape: What There Is to Recognise

i

Early on in the second act of *Waiting for Godot* Estragon, a dog-eared Beckett tramp who claims to have once been a poet ('Isn't that obvious?'), expresses considerable dismay at the *un*-inspiring prospects of what can only be described as a minimalist's *scène à faire*:

> Recognise! What is there to recognise? All my lousy life I've crawled about in the mud! And you talk to me about scenery! (*Looking wildly about him.*) Look at this muckheap! . . . You and your landscapes![1]

Although the intrepid Vladimir urges him to 'calm' himself by staying the course, critics of the play have by and large come round to Gogo's assessment of his unenviable situation on this empty performance space. '*A country road. A tree. Evening*' – the famous stage direction that sets the outdoor scene on a spare platform never dressed quite the same way before – would give even a visionary director like Peter Brook more than a moment's pause (as it did so indeed: witness his landmark productions of *King Lear* and *A Midsummer Night's Dream* for the Royal Shakespeare Company, each in its own way an energetic response to the new *Godot* scenography, the former with a menacing touch of *Endgame* in the air).[2] In Beckett's play there's a tree, of course, with – lest we forget – its well-placed leaves added surreptitiously by a conscientious stage-hand during the interval separating the not quite equally paced two acts. There's a bit more to it than that, too: a mound, a pair (or two) of shoes that don't quite fit; a radish, black; a supply of turnips; and one never-to-be-forgotten carrot that turns out to taste, well, like a carrot. Yet compared to Ibsen, one would have to admit, there's not a lot here to write home about. 'The only thing I'm sure of,' the playwright said of his players, reduced as they are to such a decrepit stage reality, 'is that they're wearing bowler hats.'[3]

Empty though it may be – but not 'empty' in the same sense the playwright will explore in his late, great works of the 1970s and 1980s – the set for *Waiting for Godot* is nonetheless filled with a material allure that is constantly seeking to redefine itself. The play 'must have', as the German director Walter Asmus once observed, 'a conceivable, real background'.[4] This is not so much a form of recognition as Aristotle discusses it in *The Poetics*; for in *Godot* the *anagnorisis* of the Greek theatre is replaced by something much more elementary but no less dramatically complex: the virtue of setting, then resetting, the landscape of the stage with things seen, then unseen, on the place Pozzo thinks might very well be 'the Board'. What there is to recognise on this diminished space might be best understood by considering the dynamics of the various landscapes struggling to impose themselves, suggestively, on the audience's imagination. These might be outlined as follows:

(i) the stark but richly articulated exterior scene we see before us on the stage;

(ii) landscapes that serve as the setting for offstage action;

(iii) pictures of some other world that can only *be* imagined; and

(iv) the landscapes from the past, which serve to illuminate the back-story the characters (more or less) remember.

Negotiations here will be very much to the point, Gogo's frustration notwithstanding.

Let us begin with 'the local situation',[5] the kinetic image of waiting Beckett creates on a single set as the curtain slowly rises on his 'twilight' drama (if indeed there is to be a curtain; Beckett was certainly thinking of one in 1953, when *Godot* opened on the intimate box set of the Théâtre de Babylone on the boulevard Raspail in Paris).[6] Positioned on stage with much precision and authority, that image will prove to be remarkably flexible, at times even unstable, as the dramatic action, such as it is, begins to unfold. Gogo and Didi repeatedly examine the haunting stage image to which this play has them tied, or rather in their case 'ti-ed'; eminent interlocutors that they are, they're suspicious, like Pozzo, even of its manufactured sky, 'qua sky'; and, like the characters in another great Irish play, Yeats's *Purgatory*, they 'study', among other things, 'that tree'.[7] And as they do so, we do so, too; the landscape, initially taken as a given, is now placed in something like sharp relief, becoming the unexpected subject of mystery, even intrigue. Those boots, once black, turn out to be brown in the second act, though perhaps, once a 'kind of grey', they're now actually a 'kind of green'. But by that time the tree, said to be a willow ('no more weeping') and later 'no use' to them 'at all', has already been transformed.

Didi scans the horizon, Gogo gazes into the distance. We watch in silence as all action is suddenly arrested, the better to evaluate the potential 'beauty of the way', if not 'the goodness of the wayfarers', as our act of *looking* is itself called into question. Dusk. 'Will night never come?' The Irish novelist John Banville called Beckett 'nothing if not an old-style landscape writer';[8] for this playwright surely knows what such staged 'twilights' can be made to do. Little wonder that great artists like Giacometti and Louis le Brocquy have been so attracted to the design elements of this landmark play.[9]

'*Enter Pozzo and Lucky*' – and, when they do so, they quite overwhelm the discreet visual threshold previously established at the beginning of each act. 'Reinforcements at last!' They bring with them such a cornucopia of material – stage props, really – that one might indeed wonder if they have inadvertently ventured on to the wrong set of the wrong play on the wrong night. And yet they quickly establish their credentials as bona fide dramatis personae for the same waiting game, members 'of the same species' fated to play their parts, over and over again, in the same rep. They do so, however, in their own individual way, this time with bags, stool, whip, rope, pipe, vaporiser, napkin, chicken bones and slobber. Lucky – Beckett said perhaps he was called Lucky because he is lucky to have 'no more expectations'[10] – has two additional tricks up his sleeve, thinking and dancing, though you will forgive me, I hope, if I present them here in reverse order. His bravura speech, the first of this play's several monologues, threatens to upstage everything, not to mention everyone else, on Beckett's stage; and his pathetic choreography in a dance called 'The Hard Stool' is an emblem for the 'net' that finally ensnares them all. Foreground invades background; how the mood has changed. The same but different, austerity is hardly the word one would use to describe the blocking on this suddenly reconfigured stage space.

An even greater instability affecting the play's atmosphere greets Gogo and Didi in Act Two, the so-said '*Next day. Same time. Same place.*' The same set of roped travelling companions also reappears, but they now move across the stage slowly and more tentatively, and from the opposite direction. Perhaps this time they have been expected by their *louche* hosts, but not in such a profoundly diminished state: Pozzo is 'as blind as fortune' and his 'knook' has been struck dumb, no explanations on offer. 'Accursed' by time ('When! When!') and haunted as much by absence as loss, the emotional resonance of this key scene upends all patterns previously established. And as the Boy, too, returns by the end of the play, telling us what we already know, that Godot will not come, not now and perhaps never, he serves as the unwitting harbinger of darkness: the moon suddenly rises, artificial yet real, as the light of day on this landscape is now literally – but also poignantly – transformed. Repeating the same line Didi used at the end of Act One, Gogo, the agent of closure for the play, makes us 'see' it now somewhat differently:

> Let's go.
> *They do not move.*
> *Curtain.*

I spend some time here emphasising this play's modest but highly flexible landscape not so much to refute Gogo – no Tom Stoppard, I, to enter into an argument with a stage character[11] – but rather to draw attention to *Godot's* remarkable visual display. In this drama Beckett recovers the representational and lyrical functions of the stage, assimilating and disarming any minimalist scepticism. Candid *and* playful, each of the work's 'little' canters calls for the *mise-en-scène* to be arranged so deftly that we hardly notice its susceptibility to instability and reinvention. 'Talk . . . about scenery!' Especially in the hands of a skilful director and a sensitive lighting designer, Beckett's set demands a heightened responsiveness to its various textures. What the play shows us is how much dramatic energy can be derived from a simple landscape, no matter how minimal the set may initially appear to be.[12]

ii

Beckett's use of offstage action has been similarly poised to 'expand' the referentiality of the play's pliant landscape, which in this case turns out to be not necessarily bleak or portentous. Although Beckett would loathe the comparison (his taste ran towards Proust, not Balzac), his technique here reveals him, oddly enough, at his most realistic and Ibsenesque.[13] For it was of course Papa Ibsen who succeeded in adapting the classical theatre's dependence on offstage action and made it function on the modern European stage. Think for a moment of Mrs Linde sitting alone on a rocking chair in *A Doll's House* as she listens anxiously to the noise of a party taking place in some other room in some other apartment, where Nora dances the tarantella; or, more Beckett-like, the sound of footfalls two elderly sisters, recently united, hear as John Gabriel Borkman paces, back and forth, in an upstairs gallery.

Godot, of course, takes considerable liberties with such a device, especially so when the single set can no longer hold the characters where they have been initially placed. Unlike Sam Shepard, who has a belligerent brother pee all over his sister's chicken in *Curse of the Starving Class,* Beckett's Vladimir runs offstage to relieve himself; and he will do so more than once. His sidekick initially observes him from afar; but on a subsequent go, this time to 'End of the corridor, on the left', he is joined in his vigil by Pozzo, who trenchantly observes, '*having put on his glasses*', 'Oh I say' (Beckett is at this point in his career by no means beyond potty humour).

Yet this play's most spectacular use of offstage action, and most puzzling, concerns nothing less than the tantalising figure of Godot himself, about whom the characters have a great deal to say. To the question, who or what is Godot, we might very well want to add this: just *where* is *his* offstage drama taking place? Didi asks the young messenger a lot of questions, but this is one he never thinks of reckoning. Does Mr Godot have a beard? Is it fair or black? (It's said to be 'white'.) Did you see two other men? What does he do, this Mr Godot? (The answer: 'nothing'.) Perhaps it was your brother came yesterday? Who minds the sheep and who minds the goats? Where do the boys sleep? Are there are in fact two of them? There's a weighty meta-question, too: just where is this 'Godin. . . Godet . . . Godot . . . anyhow you see who I mean' to be finally located? In that same ambiguous space where we don't see the goad in Beckett's *Act Without Words I*? We're a long way now from those 'great reckonings in little rooms' characteristic of Ibsen's dramaturgy.[14] Well, maybe not such a long way after all: perhaps this is really more of the same, only less.

Elsewhere in the Beckett canon the use of offstage action can be similarly effective from a dramatic point of view, but just as problematic. Clov exits the set to conduct his business in the offstage kitchen of *Endgame*, 'ten feet by ten feet by ten feet' ('Nice dimensions, nice proportions'), in a tight regimen that includes killing a rat before it dies.[15] But when he takes another journey up a ladder to look out of one of the two windows featured in this interior scene (his '*stiff, staggering walk*' never makes this easy), what he *says* he sees there cannot be certified in exactly the same way. His reported sighting of 'a small boy', a 'potential procreator' on the horizon, may very well be much less the occasion for 'an underplot' than, as Hamm suspects, pure invention. Windows, theatrically oriented, are not clear enough to see through. Something about them is closed off; they don't invite reliable vision. For Hamm in any case all dramatic action remains, so to speak, offstage: he's blind.

Krapp's duet with a tape recorder in Beckett's next play, the monologue he wrote for Patrick Magee, allows his actor to indulge in a number of unseen activities, though these are limited to the opening moments of the play, when he retreats to the grim backstage to uncork a bottle or retrieve his dusty old dictionary. Winnie, no longer cursed with a similar mobility in *Happy Days*, is of the earth 'earthy', planted as she is so majestically in a mound. Move over, Molly Bloom: here is the earth-mother figure to upstage any potential competitor, inside or outside the theatre. In the first act Winnie's worried, justifiably, about overdoing it with 'the handbag', even though this terrific prop provides her with the welcome illusion of a full day's schedule of activities. But behind that mound, and never completely seen by us, a number of peculiar activities are ongoing – and just as deliberately stagey:

> ([*Winnie*] *cranes back to look at* [*Willie*]. *Pause.*) Oh really!
> (*Pause.*) Have you no handkerchief, darling? (*Pause.*) Have
> you no delicacy? (*Pause.*) Oh, Willie, you're not eating it!
> Spit it out, dear, spit it out! (*Pause. Back front.*) Ah well,
> I suppose it's only natural. (*Break in voice.*) Human.[16]

All of this in the midst of what will be *Happy Days*'s most extended use of offstage action, this one rendered, however, as some busy time remembered. The passage of Mr Shower 'or Cooker – no matter – and the woman – hand in hand' takes place somewhere beyond the '*pompier trompe-l'oeil backcloth*' designed to represent the '*unbroken plain and sky*' that serves as the elegant but simple landscape for this second of Beckett's plays to be set, this time symmetrically, out of doors.

And yet it is the offstage action in *Waiting for Godot* that renders this playwright's landscapes most deceptively dynamic. In a bold act of hybridisation, Beckett shows his characters both on stage and off when he tightens the rope. And here I am by no means speaking figuratively. Pozzo's entrance is delayed; he is, literally, at the end of his rope. At first – and this is crucial – we see only Lucky, attached to a taut noose and moving slowly, Robert Wilson-wise, as Pozzo, a ham actor waiting in the wings, prepares for his red-carpet entrance. 'How did you find me?' he asks rather grandly later in the same scene, 'I weakened a little towards the end. Perhaps you didn't notice?' Their departure is just as strategic as they move towards that place, too, where all other Beckett characters go: ON. Pozzo takes a running leap, backwards now (it's late in the game), as the unfortunate Lucky falls on his bags, exhausted – somewhere, someplace offstage.

iii

It may come as somewhat of a surprise to discover that a dramatist so often celebrated for doing more and more with less and less should be credited with extracting so much ornate dramatic potential from such an age-old convention as offstage action. Arthur Miller correctly observed that 'a playwright like Beckett was always after a minimalist conceit',[17] although Beckett's way of achieving it generally relied on a careful analysis of just how such an image might be structured to account for the stage's specific requirements. Foremost among the techniques Beckett employs to evoke any number of additional landscapes is his firm command of the rich descriptive vocabulary built into the play's dialogue. And in *Waiting for Godot* he does this in a profoundly literary way. A rich allusive texture is there from the very opening lines, when Vladimir ponders the biblical hermeneutics of only 'one of the four' reporting that 'only one of the two' was saved. Estragon is more visually inclined. What he remembers from his catechism is the vaguely sentimentalised picture of a landscape painted in something less than bold primary colours, though impressionistic all the same:

> I remember the maps of the Holy Land. Coloured they
> were. Very pretty. The Dead Sea was pale blue. The very
> look of it made me thirsty. That's where we'll go, I used to
> say, that's where we'll go for our honeymoon. We'll swim.
> We'll be happy.

Biblical landscapes mapped out like this, of course, can only *be* imagined, however filtered they may be through centuries of depiction in Christian European painting. Beckett's characters draw upon such pictorial imagery liberally, albeit unselfconsciously; and as they do so they expand the visual range of his drama as a whole. On Golgotha 'they crucified quick'; and when Gogo compares himself to Christ, he envisions him walking barefoot, just as he plans to do. Needless to say, in this rendering both figures will not be wearing sandals – 'No laces, no laces.'

Pictures drawn from the characters' own past will be featured in even more graphic detail. The Mâcon country, which Didi wants to remember but Gogo can't or won't, was the geographic centre for this couple's grape-harvesting. In the English version of the play Didi can no longer summon up the exact name of the place, nor even recall the name of the man they worked for. In *En attendant Godot*, however, the memoir is set more circumstantially in the Vaucluse / 'Merdecluse', where the proprietor is said to have been the actual farmer, Bonnelly, Beckett worked for in Roussillon, in exchange for red wine and potatoes.[18] But how well these tramps – at least one of them – know France. In the 1890s they were among the first to climb the Eiffel Tower, 'hand in hand', although now 'they' (whoever 'they' are) wouldn't even 'let [them] up'. Pozzo, too, comes equipped with a back-story; his takes place in the big house referred to only as 'the manor'. (Beckett has a bit more to say about this in *Text 5* of *Texts for Nothing*: 'Why did Pozzo leave home, he had a castle and retainers.')[19] Fragments from other stories, past, passing or to come, are somewhat more circumscribed. Pozzo, who in his past needed one and so 'took a knook', informs Gogo and Didi that he is bound for 'the fair', where he intends to sell Lucky for a good price. But if this scene does indeed take place between the acts, the sale has apparently not gone well.

In *Endgame*, *Happy Days* and *Krapp's Last Tape* such back-stories become increasingly elaborate, providing Beckett's audience with pictures from the past that both energise and destabilise the material presence of the *mise-en-scène*, no matter how limited that initially appears to be. While Hamm's evocations are somewhat suspect – he's a chronicler *and* a fictionaliser (two strikes against him), a storyteller who uses the past as raw material for 'prolonged creative effort', thereby rendering him untrustworthy – Nell and

Nagg are likely to turn out to be much more reliable historians. They mythologise the perilous road to Sedan, where they crashed on their 'tandem' and lost their 'shanks', at the same time as they memorialise it. And they prove to be equally nostalgic about jokes and sawdust and sugarplums. Clov, by contrast, lives in the agony of this play's perpetual present; for him the earth remains 'extinguished', even though, unlike Nell and Nagg, he 'never saw it lit'. Winnie tries as hard as she can to keep such despair at bay. Lusty lady that she still is (and 'that is what I find so wonderful'), one of her principal means for doing so in *Happy Days* is to rhapsodise about other landscapes, 'to speak in the old style', where even a romantic tryst or two can take place. 'Oh the happy memories!' she waxes, then wanes. *Oh, les beaux jours* indeed . . .

   Krapp's 'case nought'[20] is perhaps even more particular. With his *aide-memoire*, 'box thrree, spool five', he can hold the favourite part of the past, his little piece of eternity, in the palm of his hand, as though his tape were the only true mnemonic of experience. The past is a retreat; Krapp goes there eagerly to shake off the cold present and the even colder future:

> Be again in the dingle on a Christmas Eve, gathering holly, the red berried. (*Pause.*) Be again on Croghan on a Sunday morning, in the haze, with the bitch, stop and listen to the bells. (*Pause.*) And so on. (*Pause*). Be again, be again.[21]

What 'remains of all that misery' is captured, habitually and for ever, on spools of recording tape: 'A girl in a shabby green coat, on a railway-station platform.' But what existence, really, does this past have? It is only what the present once was, the past that once was – if only as Krapp, the writer who once was, has chosen to remember it by giving it a shape in words. His version relies on images that soon beget other images: the place on the canal where Krapp's mother 'lay a-dying'; the 'black ball' that he will feel in his hand 'until [his] dying day'; Fanny, 'the bony old ghost of a whore'; his one attendance at Vespers, when he fell asleep and 'fell off the pew'; and finally the most enduring landscape of all, the one he switches back to again and again, spools grinding away:

> I said again I thought it was hopeless and no use going on
> and she agreed, without opening her eyes. (*Pause.*) I asked
> her to look at me and after a few moments – (*pause*) –
> after a few moments she did, but the eyes just slits, because
> of the glare. I bent over her to get them in the shadow and
> they opened. (*Pause. Low.*) Let me in. (*Pause.*) We drifted
> in among the flags and stuck. The way they went down,
> sighing before the stem! (*Pause.*) I lay down across her with
> my face in her breasts and my hand on her. We lay there
> without moving. But under us all moved, and moved us,
> gently, up and down, and from side to side.

When this play ends a few moments later, charged as it is with such a rich and evocative romantic landscape – 'The face she had! The eyes! Like . . . (*hesitates*) . . . chrysolite!' – the haunting picture of an old man alone on stage is suddenly left with what we're all left with in the end, only memories, as his 'case nought' is fatally and fatalistically transformed. Just as stage silence amplifies all that we have just heard, so it magnifies all that we now see; the slow fade-out on the seated figure provides us with both the final image and a fixed after-image. Dramatic closure like this has rarely been achieved in the theatre, nor has it ever been quite so devastating and complete: Krapp remains '*motionless staring before him*' as the '*tape runs on in silence*'. Mallarmé, who liked to think that it was only in silence that sound achieved its ideal fulfilment, would have been very pleased:[22]

Curtain.

iv

What is all the more impressive about the three major plays Beckett wrote in the decade following *Godot* is the maturity of vision he displays in developing the multiple landscapes competing for our attention on stage. Such unseen presences become, if anything, even more powerful in his late style for the theatre, where he clarifies and intensifies their dramatic implications. This is, as the playwright told the designer Jocelyn Herbert, 'work in regress with usual vanishing point in view'.[23] In the series of short plays beginning with *Not I* in 1972, the space of the stage, as I have argued elsewhere, becomes the space of human consciousness.[24] What looks abstract, after Magritte, turns out to be far less so, despite and perhaps because of the wholesale assault on a visual horizon that invites careful, lingering scrutiny from start to finish. This is, to paraphrase Porter Abbott, a landscape 'for being elsewhere'.[25] *Not I*, which divides its stage unevenly, has been cleverly arranged to thwart any easy sense of recognition, featuring immediacy instead. The play relegates the minimal image of Mouth to one side, the maximal image of Auditor to the other, setting perspective askew. But before long even Mouth's fantastic tirade, which from a structural point of view continues where Lucky's speech ends, depends on a series of realistic vignettes ('live scene[s]', the author called them),[26] including an innocent visit to a 'supermart', an appearance in court before a judge and an ominous sexual assault, 'face in the grass' (Beckett said he was not thinking of a rape scene, though his text seems to think otherwise).[27] The atlas here may have been fractured, but realistic landscapes, no matter how fragmentary, continue to assert themselves, as though the pendulum was swinging back towards narrative expression. In Beckett this doesn't mean a full-scale restoration of mimetic or gestural conventions, but it does mean a return to narrative, more implicit than explicit, and, within the storyline, the interactions of theatrically articulated characters.

Not I does not so much tell stories as allude to them, as though to hint at mysteries. The play doesn't show us so much as suggest narrative fragments, inviting us to join them in the act of creation through the process of our own perception.[28] Beckett conveys his theatricality through the less rationally explicit but the more emotionally complicit means of Auditor's movement and Mouth's image. And a similar technique can be observed in the piece its author called 'the brother to *Not I*',[29] *That Time* – a bold work that is at once both introverted and expressive. A stark, disembodied head is suspended on stage and positioned slightly off centre as voices A, B and C recycle the plenitude of events summing up a life now spent, though perhaps not well. However unspecified – in *Footfalls* that dreadful *un-* will become even more startling and significant – there's always a story here, and a back-story, too, accompanied, as in *Othello*, by a momentous 'world of sighs'.[30] The church door in *Footfalls*, the 'other only windows' in *Rockaby*, the Isle of Swans in *Ohio Impromptu*, and giving someone 'the works' offstage in *What Where*,[31] that same place where the Director is hidden in *Catastrophe*, enlarge each play's scenic dimension and exoticise it, so to speak, rendering all stylistic limitations lame. What Beckett actually allows us to see in the minimal images arranged so precisely on 'the Board' may be merely a small sample of what might be lurking in this stage darkness, sight unseen.

Other works, especially those written for television, advance dream landscapes where, as in Strindberg, characters sometimes 'evaporate, crystallise, scatter and converge. But a single consciousness holds sway over them all – that of the dreamer.'[32] Like Strindberg's, Beckett's is a highly restricted, even liminal world, but it flashes in and out, as in a dream. In plays like . . . *but the clouds . . .* , *Ghost Trio* and *Nacht und Träume*, which brings screen life to a dream within a dream, technology wears a distinctly human face, even though the characters such technology displays seem to have a quiet fear of disappearing without a trace – not gone perhaps, 'but definitely on Death Row'.[33] Exploiting the enormous potential of camera angles and especially film editing, one visionary landscape can even superimpose itself on another: a scrim-like woman's face suddenly appears, lingers, then disappears on the already illusory screen image in . . . *but the clouds* . . . ; and in *Nacht und Träume* a 'helping hand'[34] and a handkerchief, always just beyond focus, materialise from some upper realm beyond, loaded with possible symbolism, as though the whole enterprise were some sort of modernist take on *The Annunciation* by Fra Filippo Lippi or a delicate fresco by Fra Angelico.

Disembodied heads that fade in and out, as in the TV version of *What Where*, a drama well named for the purposes of this discussion, seem to take us a long way from what there is to recognise in *Waiting for Godot*. And yet the landscape of that early play, empty as it is, is everywhere filled with mysterious suggestion as Beckett builds upon any number of stage conventions to assert his own authority on a genre always begging to be reinvented. One of the principal ways he does so as his work progresses is to make us see even in things unseen the vastness of a universe seeking representation on a lonely stage. Gogo, like the rest of us, might be heartily encouraged to look a bit more thoroughly into the void. There may be – well, in fact there is, as this 'talk' about 'landscapes'[35] seeks to demonstrate – a lot more *going on* there than meets the naked eye.

But that is perhaps enough, for the time being at least, of what Malone calls – as well *we* might – 'all this fucking scenery'.[36]

CHAPTER 4

Beckett's Shades of the Colour Grey

i

Grey, greyness, greying – grey as a verb, as a noun, as an adjective, as a process – evoke an enigmatic world that is neutral and unstable, an intermediate zone fading from darkness to light, then suddenly back again. An endpoint that is always on the verge of becoming something else again, grey is both a beginning and an end, diminution as well as potential, ashes but also fertile – very fertile – grey matter. Place a palette of greys next to any item of another colour, as Beckett does – a few leaves, a blood-stained handkerchief, a carrot, a mouth, a banana – and its weary hues come alive with an unsuspected dynamism, a 'less' that has quickly turned into quite a bit more. An imperfect *lessness* at best (depending on how you look at it), grey, when it stands stoutly and proudly on its own, can also be more than enough to sustain an entire fictional world.

In Beckett's work grey, the colour grey, becomes a vast serial motif in a wide range of genres. Mixtures of black and white, shades of the colour grey bring a variety of tonal values to his writing, and the different properties he assigns to them display a subtle coordination of rich textual and theatrical effects. Beckett's shades of the colour grey everywhere encourage spatial, visual, even narrative ambiguity, and their conditional states stretch across subject, object, image, temporality and indeed over the colour grey itself. In the accomplished fiction of his productive middle period, the bold and uncompromising novels popularly known as the trilogy (*Molloy*, *Malone Dies* and *The Unnamable*), grey is thematised as a grim but sometimes hilarious state of consciousness, one that more often than not provides some rough descriptive terrain: 'a little yes, a little no, enough to exterminate a regiment of dragoons'.[1] Vocabulary is at a premium here as it literally fires away. Grey is at 'first murky, then frankly opaque', 'dimly transparent', then 'literally sparkling at times', except 'in so far as this kind of grey may be called a colour'. Rarely has the coordination of shades been so powerfully evocative of an entire field of limited possibility; and, in this restricted arena, 'All remains grey, it's the grey we need.' 'Silence' itself is 'stunted as grey', and the shadow it casts 'means' – figuratively and provocatively – 'nothing'. A 'narrow grey sky' reduces the very tides, imagistically, to a 'slow grey'. It's 'a nice grey', however, 'of the kind recommended as going with everything'. Such a 'greyish concoction', on the other hand, can also prove ominous, 'meant to be depressing no doubt', causing any narrator, Beckett's included, to fall 'prey' to 'delusions' at those bleak moments when 'he suffers from the grey'. Note how the sun doesn't shine here, even as it does, having no similar 'alternative', on *Murphy*'s comparatively radiant 'nothing new'.[2] Still, from time to time 'this grey is shot with rose, like the plumage of certain birds'. And it can also give rise to sharp visual stimulation just when we least expect to find it; a Beckett text can make us 'see grey, like still smoke, unbroken'. 'Yes' – what's that endearing affirmation doing here? – 'no doubt one may speak of grey, personally I have no objection.'

But speaking of grey is not the same thing as framing it, materially, within a convincing dramatic display. And it is here that Beckett's originality and forcefulness as a writer for the European stage can be more fully appreciated and understood. Theatre is, above all else, a 'seeing place' – that's the public sphere ancient Greek *theatron* points us to. Sitting in a theatre watching shades of grey, however, and for any length of time, can be – as we might expect – downright boring. Beckett is of course not alone in confronting this dilemma. Playwrights before him, most notably that great Russian modernist Chekhov, have always had to reconfigure monotony – and here I use the word quite deliberately – to meet the demands and stubborn conventions of what is always going to be a highly stylised performance space. The challenge here is to liberate grey (and in Beckett's case 'Grey rather than white, a pale shade of grey'[3]) – its colour, its atmosphere, its mood, its likely effects – from tired, even sentimental associations.

The problem with grey is that grey, as the French might say, is *triste*; or as we might say in Italian to describe the ill wind that brings bad weather, metaphorical or otherwise, grey marks the sinking depression of any *giornata grigia* (we can say this in English, too – 'a grey day' – but somehow the Italian language puts a lot more into it). Little wonder marketers prefer to hawk variations on the colour grey as silver or platinum, even chrome (Frank Gehry's luminous 'titanium' would perhaps be even more saleable in today's consumerist culture). Shakespeare himself was not above employing such circumlocutions; he has his Horatio, for example, abandon the pallor of grey to describe the dead King Hamlet's beard 'as I have seen it in his life, / A sable silver'd'.[4] In theatre language a simple grey beard, by comparison, just doesn't cut it.

Enlivening grey would therefore seem to be for the playwright a full-time job; but it is a task Beckett wholeheartedly embraces in his exploration of new dramatic forms in new dramatic contexts. These can be highly elliptical in the plays he composed in the last two decades of his life; but their outline is already visible in his signature work of the early 1950s, *Waiting for Godot*, his most Chekhovian play. Waiting around in the waning light for something to arrive that never comes, especially when the grey evening vigil is staged on a dusty country road in front of a lifeless tree – there's a memorable rock, too – hardly seems like the most promising of dramatic situations until Pozzo reminds us that 'You don't know what our twilights can do.'[5] Pozzo's moments of fading light are intermediate periods of time, unclear zones of diminishing daylight that also signify blurred images of ever-greying space. Chekhov, attached as he is to the materiality of fourth-wall realism, likes to ratchet it up with the intrusion of lovesick majors, bored young wives who whistle or valorise pens, ageing Lotharios who collect bouquets of beautiful, mournful roses, and lovelorn sixteen-year-olds who take snuff because they're in mourning for their lives. Yet his characters, like Beckett's, are suspended – stuck, more likely – in the same unenviable place, if only they knew it: a grey area best perceived as a middle, a muddle and an end – and one that is at best inconclusive. Sugarplums, running out, will be of no use to any of them, nor will Chekhov's endless cups of tea, as the samovar boils away.

Abstracting, highlighting really, the grey area that is at once *Godot*'s narrative focus and the potent physical atmosphere that makes us envision it, bringing its spontaneity to stage life, Beckett's formal symmetry can be daunting. It is also something that can be easily missed. A Beckett text is tough; it defies any number of attempts to destabilise its structure by turning it into the representation of some alternative reality its efficient dramaturgy swiftly rejects. Yearning for definition without being able to find it is, of course, Beckett's well-travelled ground zero. And in this respect grey – the colour grey – is the perfect analogue. One cannot imagine *Waiting for Godot* having the same impact in any other colour.

On Beckett's stage, then, the use of monochrome, shades of grey, becomes a highly elaborate decorative motif, creating multiple shadow effects that offset the reduced dimensions of the colour scheme. Luxuriating in the colour grey, the drama as it develops becomes a virtual discourse on this most fragile of all shades. 'They were a kind of grey,' Gogo laments, missing the lost boots he originally thought might have been slightly black. Didi tries to comfort him with a different pair that at first aperçu seem to be nothing like them. 'These are brown,' Gogo complains bitterly (and, as an afterthought, 'Well, they're a kind of green'). 'Your boots,' Didi despairs, 'what are you going to do with your boots?' Beckett's tramps will make much of them. Estragon, *semper fidelis*, refuses to wear any other colour; since the grey ones can't be found, he'll go barefoot instead, just like Christ. 'You're not going to compare yourself to Christ!' Didi bellows, followed by Gogo's petulant response: 'All my life I've compared myself to him.' Now there's a grey area indeed. On this set 'everything oozes', nothing glows, and the moon itself is said to be, ironising Shelley, 'pale for weariness' ('of climbing heaven' and having to gaze on the likes of two such misfits). Mr Godot's beard is similarly poised somewhere between one extreme and another, albeit offstage. Vladimir enquires in some dismay: 'Fair or . . . (*he hesitates*) . . . or black?' 'I *think* it's white, Sir' (emphasis mine), is the boy's tentative response – only marginally more assured than the refrain he (and perhaps his brother, too) uses elsewhere: 'I don't know, Sir.'

In Beckett's next play, *Endgame*, shades of the colour grey darken, rendering them even more stark and profound. The playwright described the work as being 'as dark as ink'.[6] Here Beckett is under increasing pressure to make his deepening shades dramatically viable. (You don't go to a play like this expecting to celebrate the diversions of a colour wheel; think of Jessica Tandy's candour after she played Mouth in the world premiere of *Not I*: 'I'd like to do a musical next.'[7]) *Endgame* opens on a '*bare interior*' featuring '*two ashbins*'; the spare set is illuminated by a piercing '*grey light*'.[8] Hamm's '*very red face*', as tortured as any in a portrait by Francis Bacon, is the single element disturbing the insistent monotone established in the opening '*brief tableau*': two characters frozen in stage space for a few weighty seconds of stage time. And the rising action culminates in Clov's big moment, a grim peroration that has the shape if not the release of some empowering climactic speech:

I open the door of the cell and go. I am so bowed I only see my feet, if I open my eyes, and between my legs a little trail of black dust. I say to myself that the earth is extinguished, though I never saw it lit.

(*Pause.*)

It's easy going.

(*Pause.*)

When I fall I'll weep for happiness.

Along the way Beckett uses a number of elements to extend and enhance the rigorous atmosphere of his play, distrusting the sublimity of white but similarly undermining the otherwise dire and definitive consequences associated with black. 'Damn the sun' – though it's not quite night; on the artifice of this playing space, this 'board', such things can be neither confirmed nor denied. In *Endgame* light is merely 'sunk', there's no certain 'ray of sunshine', and Clov tells Hamm that what little 'white' remains is 'not more than usual'.

Even the props on this set are compromised. The blind Hamm revels in the thought that his stuffed three-legged dog, imperfect and unfinished though it is – 'the sex goes on in the end' – is nonetheless pure white, though we see things differently (it's nothing of the kind). 'Leave him there, imploring me.' Mother Pegg 'died of darkness' – a condition on a sliding scale – not the dark, and Clov yearns but fails to achieve his dream: 'A world where all would be silent and still and each thing in its last place, under the last dust.' The gulls he says he sees outside this perilous shelter are neither black nor conclusively white, shaded as they are in the same indeterminate way as the 'sails of the herring fleet'; and Nagg's longed-for pap – 'Me pap! . . . I want me pap!' (a bland mixture that is anything but nourishing) – is just as vaguely discoloured (and like so many other things in this play, it too has run out). There's no more pain-killer; but there's an awful lot of grey on the horizon. Clov climbs a ladder to look out on a window to the world; he reports that what he sees through his telescope is also, and not surprisingly:

> Grey.
> (*Lowering the telescope, turning towards Hamm, louder.*)
> Grey!
> (*Pause. Still louder.*)
> GRREY!
> (*Pause. He gets down, approaches Hamm from behind, whispers in his ear.*)
> **Hamm** (*startling*) Grey! Did I hear you say grey?
> **Clov** Light black. From pole to pole.
> **Hamm** You exaggerate.

ii

There is certainly no exaggerating the sombre world we encounter in *Krapp's Last Tape*, where the decorative motif of Krapp's dismal den has been done up for the past thirty years in unappealing shades of the colour grey. Set in 'a late evening in the future', the scene opens on the seated figure of a 'wearish old man', 'unshaven', with 'disordered grey hair'.[9] Discovered at his desk in an area of 'strong white light', the rest of the stage in darkness, he is about to prepare himself and his microphone for the annual ritual of tape-recording the past year's non-events. Krapp at sixty-nine is now an audience to his own life, no longer an actor in it. His will be a low-grade fade-out.

Krapp's Last Tape represents a considerable advance in Beckett's theatricalisation of vast shades of the colour grey. As James Knowlson has pointed out, the drama in this case reaches for its stage life through a steady oscillation between rhythmic figurations of darkness and light.[10] These can extend even to the minutest of details, as when Krapp listens to a tape of his voice made three decades before and recalls an even earlier time when he lived with Bianca (*white*) on Kedar Street (Hebrew for a configuration resembling something like *black*). This is the very same tape that preserves his memory of a nurse, 'all white and starch', a 'dark beauty' with big breasts and 'a big black hooded perambulator, most funereal thing'. It also gives us the details of his fascination with holding a celebrated 'black ball' he will 'feel . . . in [his] hand until [his] dying day'; he might have kept it, but he 'gave it' instead to a 'little white dog'.

And then there is of course the play's opening scene, when Krapp consults a dusty old dictionary about the word *viduity* and reads on to find 'the vidua or weaver bird', 'black plumage of male'. Details like this quickly accumulate to advance the play's unpredictable mixture of the morbid with the downright, then the bitterly comic. A confirmed drunk, and becoming progressively more so as the recording session runs its interrupted course, Krapp performs a solo rendition of the Protestant hymn he sang at Vespers ('Went to sleep and fell off the pew'). And the second time he does so his voice is hoarse and heavy with the brutal irony of the present:

> Now the day is over,
> Night is drawing nigh-igh,
> Shadows – (*coughing, then almost inaudible*) – of the evening
> Steal across the sky.

Although, in his study of that 'bastard' Proust, Beckett notes that memory 'presents the past in monochrome',[11] that is not how things happen in *Krapp's Last Tape*. Tenderly sheltered in 'box three', the descriptive landscape detailed on 'spool five' is rife with a rhetoric of robust colour that forms a vigorous contretemps to the stage's forbidding here and now. Krapp listens, as we listen; and for one brief moment we 'see' with him a glimpse of the bright world he foolishly left behind, one in which there might have been, even for him, 'a chance of happiness':

What remains of all that misery? A girl in a shabby green coat, on a railway-station platform.

And later, in the less than luminous present fuelled by alcohol, his annotation to the passage he has just been listening to pinpoints how nostalgia can be suddenly transformed into something far more sinister, an all but debilitating perception of acute and monumental loss:

Be again in the dingle on a Christmas eve, gathering the holly, the red-berried. (*Pause.*) Be again on Croghan on a Sunday morning, in the haze, with the bitch, stop and listen to the bells. (*Pause.*) And so on. (*Pause.*) Be again, be again.

At the close of this play, when the tape runs on to the crackling sound of silence, Krapp still yearns to re-register his 'last' male 'fancies' of the girl in the punt. He now hears the favoured and highly erotic passage on 'box three, spool five' more poignantly than ever before, as the vastness of a new kind of silence, this time deadly, fatally encroaches on his diminishing grey space:

Pause. Krapp's lips move. No sound.
Past midnight. Never knew such silence. The earth might be uninhabited.
Pause.
Here I end this reel. Box – (*pause*) – three, spool (*pause*) – five. (*Pause.*) Perhaps my best years are gone. When there was a chance of happiness. But I wouldn't want them back. Not with the fire in me now. No, I wouldn't want them back.

Against such a raw background of so many shades of the colour grey, the contrast Beckett establishes here between the past and the present, between the past as it might have been lived and the past lethally downloaded on a reel, could not be rendered in a single image more theatrically concise.

When Beckett directed *Krapp's Last Tape* in 1969 at the Schiller-Theater Werkstatt in Berlin, and later in his several encounters with the work as director or as adviser to the director of this play, he made a number of modifications to his original script.[12] Many of these, like the excision of Krapp's clownish 'purple nose' and his 'surprising pair of dirty white boots, size ten at least, very narrow and pointed', as well as the overdoing it in the famous mime with the banana, have the effect of toning-down the work's risky comic business. Though every one of these changes is of considerable interest to Beckett scholars around the world, they may not always be in the best interests of the play. In performance *Krapp's Last Tape* works its way through the orchestration of many contrasts, through a rich interplay of inflected and uninflected surfaces. It is the tempo of Beckett's language, at times lyrical, but at others prosaic and comic, even broadly comic, that brings colour and movement – and drama – to the set's unforgiving shades of grey. 'This is not boring you I hope' – Didi's aside early on in *Godot* – must finally be taken at something much more than metatheatrical face value, as something that goes to the heart of the matter concerning how a play like this might hold an audience and come alive in performance. One of the great strengths of *Krapp's Last Tape* is the way in which its competing textures, those on tape and those that call for action and – even more so – swift reaction by the actor stranded alone on a relatively empty stage, reach for supremacy, finally succumbing to the rugged sobriety of the climactic moment when, like the piercing light of day, '*the tape runs on in silence*'. Diminuendo: that is the play's final, sombre journey. The rest is white noise.

iii

Happy Days may be something of an anomaly in this context, and not only because it is the first of Beckett's works to be composed for virtuoso performance by a strong female lead. Here the scene is set under '*blazing light*' that reveals a '*trompe-l'oeil backcloth*' designed to foster the illusion of '*unbroken plain and sky receding to meet in the far distance*'.[13] Although Winnie's mound is built – and in the second act rebuilt – of earth (not to be mistaken for sand), everything else we see has been calculated to achieve an unearthly '*maximum of simplicity and symmetry*'. This is a set with no shadows. Under the immense glare of a merciless, unruly sun, what *Happy Days* features instead is the blurring, the shading and the greying of memory. So many other things on Winnie's pale pile of earth disappear, run out or simply burn up; yet these stubborn gradations of memory insist on staying put, at least in 'part'. And 'that is what I find so wonderful,' Winnie waxes, then wanes, 'a part remains, of one's classics, to help one through the day'. 'What is that wonderful line,' she declaims elsewhere, 'laughing wild . . . something something laughing wild amid severest woe.' Is this what Yeats had in mind for 'the foul rag-and-bone shop of the heart'?[14] Winnie would probably spoil his poems, too, just as she mangles so many others, even when the lyric has been designed to be far less lofty:

> What are those exquisite lines? (*Pause.*) Go forget me why should something o'er that something shadow fling . . . go forget me . . . why should sorrow . . . brightly smile . . . go forget me . . . never hear me . . . sweetly smile . . . brightly sing . . . (*Pause.* [And this time] *With a sigh.*)

For Beckett's protagonist in *Happy Days*, the synapses aren't quite as sharp as they used to be, if in fact they ever were; he told the director Shivaun O'Casey 'not to make [her] too capable a woman'.[15] Yet the frailty of memory, its fractures, its failures and the unpredictable way it chooses to come and go, is nevertheless a heavy blow. Winnie – Win, 'an interrupted being'[16] – never wavers, however, in her attempt to refashion memory's seductive allure. Hers is a search for emotional validity in a variety of shapes, moods and reconstituted verbal tropes. These might be best described as private visions of her past recaptured, shards of memory that may be nothing more than vain imaginings; and yet they are discoloured by the dialogue's most compelling and enduring shadows:

> My first ball! (*Long pause.*) My second ball! (*Long pause. Closes eyes.*) My first kiss! (*Pause. Willie turns page. Winnie opens eyes.*) A Mr Johnson, or Johnston, or perhaps I should say John*stone*. Very bushy moustache, very tawny. (*Reverently.*) Almost ginger! (*Pause.*) Within a toolshed, though whose I cannot conceive. We had no toolshed and he most certainly had no toolshed.

And then all at once the mood changes:

> (*Closes eyes.*) I see the pile of pots. (*Pause.*) The tangles of bast. (*Pause.*) The shadows deepening among the rafters.

iv

As has been previously noted, the seed image for *Happy Days* bears an uncanny resemblance to the final frames in *Un Chien andalou* (1928), Buñuel's iconic work in which bodies are similarly buried up to the waist, the same position in which Winnie is planted 'up to her diddies' when the curtain rises on Beckett's play. *An Andalusian Dog*, as the movie is known in English, is a marvel of black-and-white invention. The film reveals its *noir*-ish temperament through a compilation of odd angles, sinister shadows and the strategic use of silence; the logistics consist of recording a wide range of shades of the colour grey set against a flickering light that is always on the verge of extinction. Technical choices like these will have enormous repercussions on Beckett's work as he begins to set his sights on writing plays for the mechanical media.

Beckett responded favourably to the invitation by the Evergreen Theatre at Grove Press to work on the project that became known as the 22-minute 'comic and unreal' *Film,* shot in 35mm black and white.[17] His biographers have carefully traced his early interest in Eisenstein's pioneering cinematography, and any reader of Beckett soon picks up on his fascination with the giants of the silent silver screen (Chaplin's poignant vaudeville, it hardly needs pointing out here, leaves its mark all over *Godot*).[18] In this prolific genre, as in black-and-white still photography, it is difficult to tell if grey is a distillation of many colours or a saturation of all of them. A sly demonstration of the many shades of a colour we thought we knew only too well, such celluloid splendour urges us to look closer, then to look again. Beckett's *Film* begins the inquisition with a close-up shot of an all-seeing eye.

In Beckett's work for film and television, grey is hugely generative and alive with a nervous energy. In *Film,* for example, its vast resources are always hiding in plain sight – a cat, a dog, a fish, a charcoal sketch, a chair, a torn window shade, a basket of flowers that topples over, snapshots from the past, a whistle, a wall, a pince-nez, Keaton's familiar pork-pie hat – as though they were struggling all the time to evade a threatening interiority. In this work grey gives each image its wholeness, and each shot is deployed for its singular values, resulting in a frenzied visual panorama where individual items display distinct personalities. In *Film* E (eye) and O (object) play an elaborate game of cat-and-mouse until the final, fatal investment. This occurs when the animated camera lens, the eye above all other eyes, moves in to execute a *coup-de-grâce.* Keaton's elusive face expresses panic, cauterised as it is in a full frontal exposure that registers what we have suspected all along, that $E = O$ – something like a *grey* thought in a *grey* shade. To be suddenly perceived like this is an agony of self-referential self-consciousness. 'Thought is not coloured,' as the painter Bruce Nauman once observed. 'Colour adds nothing to thought. Thought is black, white and grey.'[19]

In his plays for television Beckett discovered even greater potential for clarifying the intensity of the colour grey. The effect can be hypnotic; and what might have been merely monotonous now seems rich and full of nuance as recorded human voices transmit other-worldly sounds that evoke the passage of time: 'When I thought of her it was always night.' Much of this comes together for him in the three-part programme he called 'Shades', broadcast on the BBC in April 1977. The project consisted of an adaptation of *Not I*, Billie Whitelaw's reprise of her powerful Royal Court performance from four years before, and two new works written specifically for the medium. In *Ghost Trio* and . . . *but the clouds* . . . light, sound, movement and gesture are carefully calibrated, concentrated and suggestive, and it is through their vivid interactions that they achieve their emotional quality and dramatic appeal.

Here the renunciation of polychromy and bright hues in favour of chiaroscuro highlights a visual abstinence that allows Beckett's viewer to focus on *disegno* as opposed to *colore*. The overall grey field on a restrained television screen capable of displaying so many other colour schemes commands our attention and evokes interiority through its distinctively muted palette. And the sharp intrusion of silvery greys allows Beckett to thematise and spatialise memory in specifically visual terms: 'When I thought of her it was always night,'[20] followed by a sequence of images that *inscribe* memory rather than merely describe it. Such a vigorous eye for grey offers the camera an unlimited capacity to screen a series of motifs and recurring images, allusions and associations, through a refracted pattern of accumulation, repetition and self-quotation as a 'voice' comes 'to one in the dark':[21]

> The light: faint, omnipresent. No visible source. As if all
> luminous. Faintly luminous. No shadow. (*Pause.*) The
> colour: none. All grey. Shades of grey. (*Pause.*) The colour
> grey if you wish, shades of the colour grey. (*Pause.*) Forgive
> my stating the obvious. (*Pause.*) Keep that sound down.
> (*Pause.*) Now look closer.

In an earlier piece for television, *Eh Joe*, grey sustains the multiple valences of silence as the camera makes its 'nine slight moves in towards face, say four inches each time'. Here Beckett reveals his metaphorical and anti-metaphorical strategies when he places us both inside and outside a head to the accompaniment of a relentless voice-over, everything neatly framed in a box. *Ghost Trio* and *. . . but the clouds . . .* – where the dominant spectral motif is the scrim and the metamorphosis of shadow – further energise the complex deployment of grey as the gateway to an intimate world 'within'. And *Nacht und Träume* will be similarly monochromatic, for this, too, is staged in the same grey zone where night and dreams take place.

V

Seeking to locate dramatic assertiveness through the steady animation of a subtle and restricted plane, Beckett's plays for the mechanical media by no means stand alone as a separate investigation of the use of grey across various genres. He was never entirely sure, for example, when he finished *What Where* (*Quoi où* in French) whether he had written a play for television or a piece for live performance (and in what remains a rare instance for him, he allowed the script to be presented – to be given 'the works', that is – in both forms[22]). For Beckett, theatre, like television, is always a hypothetical space; but unlike television, theatre demands to be inhabited by actors in real as opposed to recorded time. What is perhaps most impressive about Beckett's plays for film and television is the way he adapts their technical efficiencies and reconfigures them for use in live performance space. This is especially noticeable in a reconsidered sense of the role lighting and sound play as these crucial elements contribute to the arrangement of a new concept for images that his late drama brings to the stage.

In short works like *Come and Go* and *Play* Beckett's dour palette is already dense and nothing if not secure. In both dramas sharp lighting is skilfully employed to illuminate complex representations of irony and elegy. In *Play*, in particular, a sharp beam of inquisitorial light takes centre stage as a character in its own right, prompting three pale figures buried in dark grey urns to recite their prepared texts, '*faces so lost to age and aspect as to seem almost part of urns*'. In this work bright light adds monumentality and great functionality to the shades of grey, opening up a succession of perspectives and passing spatial visualisations as the swift pacing moves from one speaker to the next. And in *Come and Go* high density light is similarly conspiratorial as it provokes yet another play of shadows. Whatever their metaphorical implications, the rings Beckett's three sisters feel on their hands at close of play only make dramatic sense if and when sharp stage lighting captures their glare. But it is in the series of works beginning with *Not I* and *That Time* that the influence of Beckett's work in the mechanical media on his stage plays can be felt most strongly, resulting in an even more nuanced role for his shades of the colour grey.

The brightly lit figure of Mouth in *Not I* has been the subject of so much critical commentary that we sometimes forget that on stage her (its?) luminous presence is matched by the elongated stature of Auditor, '*sex undeterminable*' and '*fully faintly lit*'. Dressed – '*enveloped*' is the word Beckett uses – from head to foot in a loose black djellaba, and further shrouded by a hood, the silent Auditor absorbs faint light and then displays its vague conundrum as a mysterious grey that runs the gamut from off-white to near black, with a focus on several ambiguous shades in between. The sensational evocation of two such shocking images on an otherwise blank stage, stationed literally in place for maximum contrast in mood, blocking, size, sound and silence – Mouth's '... what? ... who? ... no! .. she! .. SHE!' and Auditor's four brief movements of 'helpless compassion' – is both a tribute to the precision of televisual imagery and a tyrannical demonstration of what strange things can happen to certain elements of drama as they cross over from one genre to another. In *That Time*, which the playwright called 'the brother to *Not I*', a disembodied head, *'ten feet above stage level midstage off centre'*, seems to float in an unspecified stage darkness that first looks grey, then greyer, then greyest. Listener's old white face with *'long flaring white hair as if seen from above outspread'* serves to heighten the spectral quality of the piece as a whole. And the visions of the past broadcast by the offstage voices of A, B and C that haunt Listener are hardly more promising, cast as they are in disturbing images of ruin, stone, slabs, rubble, nettles and dirt.

Footfalls, the play Beckett wrote with Billie Whitelaw in mind, may give us the clearest example of how this technical precision in the evocation of shades of the colour grey works visually and thematically in the late drama. For in this short piece even the dialogue is paradigmatic of the image passing before our eyes:

> The semblance. (*Pause.* [*May*] *resumes pacing. After two lengths* [*she*] *halts facing front at R. Pause.*) The semblance. Faint, though by no means invisible, in a certain light. (*Pause.*) Given the right light. (*Pause.*) Grey rather than white, a pale shade of grey. (*Pause.*) Tattered. (*Pause.*) A tangle of tatters.

May, a grey figure with *'dishevelled grey hair'*, paces 'to and fro' on a lean strip of light in a *'worn grey wrap hiding feet, trailing'*, her expression intensely concentrated and attentive. The lighting here is dim, *'strongest at floor level, less on body, least on head'*. No trailing clouds of glory here. And when the value of metaphor does intrude into May's monologue, 'it all' powerfully shadows the entire known world, like the greyest of evening skies:

> Watch it pass – (*pause*) – watch her pass before the
> candelabrum, how it flames, their light . . . like moon
> through passing rack. (*Pause.*)

May's disappearance at the end of the play – '*No trace of May*' – the sound of a chime '*even a little fainter still*', is an all too brief light-and-sound show, the slow '*Fade out*' that is this earth's ultimate extinguisher: '*Hold ten seconds.*' Less, then less, then even less.

In the plays that follow, *A Piece of Monologue*, *Ohio Impromptu*, *Rockaby* and later *Catastrophe*, Beckett continues to explore the multidimensionality of grey as sophisticated technology literally brings it to light in unpredictable ways, making us rethink the nature of abstraction and the materiality of grey itself as a language for the stage. *A Piece of Monologue* tightly frames in a box set a diaphanous image that is 'on all sides nowhere', 'unutterably faint'. Props on this set, globe and pallet, are '*barely visible*'. And in this '*faint diffuse light*' the Speaker's white hair, white nightgown and white socks, as well as the white foot of his bed – all 'once white to take faint light' – are robbed of the sublimity, purity and innocence usually associated with such an unadulterated state. The Speaker's self-sustaining monologue is unnervingly self-descriptive as he intones 'slow fade up of a faint form. Out of the dark.' His is a world of phantom grey figures, of the same Greystones where Beckett's parents lie buried:

> Nothing stirring. Faintly stirring. Thirty thousand nights
> of ghosts beyond. Beyond the black beyond. Ghost light.
> Ghost nights. Ghost rooms. Ghost graves. Ghost . . . he all
> but said ghost loved ones.

A mere thirty seconds before the end of speech the palest of light from the skull-sized white globe, 'milkwhite' elsewhere, begins to fail. Its insufficiency goes unnoticed by the motionless figure staring – where else? – 'beyond'. In the background one can almost hear Giacometti cheering his famous dictum as slowly fading light closes in on this drama for being elsewhere: 'Grey! Grey! Grey!'[23]

Other phantom figures are spectacularly isolated and diminished in *Rockaby* and *Ohio Impromptu*. In one, a 'prematurely old' woman with 'unkempt grey hair' is dressed in 'best black' and sits 'subdued' in a merciless rocking chair, 'unaffected by successive fades'. In the other, two inscrutable figures in white wigs, '*as alike in appearance as possible*', sit at a plain deal table wearing identical black coats; one reads aloud while the other listens, taking stock of the pitch and masterful cadence of every word (as Hamm says, 'Every man his speciality'). In both plays sound and voice and intonation – in the one case live *and* recorded (consider W's plaintive, fitful cries for 'More'), in the other hauntingly, even alarmingly responsive and alert – are adjusted for pinpoint precision, as though with every breath they were mechanically enhanced. Reader's text chisels in stone a tale of loss he recites with appropriately grave inflection: 'Stay where we were so long alone together, my shade will comfort you.' Lighting is icy, cold and subdued, and colours the set with its chilling atmosphere of introspection: 'Thoughts, no, not thoughts. Profounds of mind. Buried in who knows what profounds of mind.'

In this grey context another play, *Catastrophe*, might be read as a crash course in just how the stage organises and accommodates itself to such a stark Beckettian landscape. 'Like the look of him?' the Assistant's opening line, initiates the several choices made by her Director, the fur-clad micromanager who seeks to control every action of the silent Protagonist. The image is very much in the making as a tortured figure stands before us incomplete, shivering and barefoot on a plinth. Adjustments are in order:

D Colour?

A Ash.

(*D takes out a cigar.*)

D Light.

(*A returns, lights the cigar, stands still. D smokes.*)

How's the skull?

A You've seen it.

D I forget.

(*A moves towards P.*)

Say it.

A Moulting. A few tufts.

D Colour?

A Ash.

(*Pause.*)

Fortunately, 'Luke's around'; and it is finally this temperamental techie who makes the necessary adjustments to darken the set, highlight 'just the head', and isolate the figure even further. The greyness is now all-encompassing, a rich middle tone full of shading and – with the aid of intense stage lighting – full of surprising variations. The Assistant 'make[s] a note'.

Beckett was delighted when the technical staff he worked with in Stuttgart on the television play *Quad* ran its bright colours of red, yellow, blue and white through a compatibility monitor to see what the piece would look like for those viewing it on black-and-white rather than colour TV. 'Marvellous,' he said. 'It's 100,000 years later.'[24] That dramatic gesture in shades of the colour grey, an adventure, really – like so much else in 'the grey dust of words' that constitutes the vast Beckett canon – is not only an exploration of practical theatre technology, but a product of a long metaphysical journey where the literal and the conceptual overlap, intermingle, and finally come to rest in the making of new and provocative stage images. And in this context grey is more ominous and threatening than black – 'Finished . . . nearly finished' – loaded as it is with ever more daunting instabilities. 'No colour, no colour,' Beckett was fond of telling his actors.[25] And no wonder Jasper Johns, pursuing a similar path disproving the law of diminishing returns in his remarkable series of grey paintings, recognised a kindred spirit when he called his 2005 oil and encaustic painting on wood with objects (two panels) 'Beckett'. 'No matter which way you turn,' the playwright said, explaining why he chose the same artist's etching of flagstones as the endpaper for a special limited edition of *Foirades/Fizzles*, 'you always come up against a stone wall.'[26] That should come as no surprise; for stones, too, like the walls they make, always come in a wide variety of shades of the colour grey.

CHAPTER 5

The Seated Figure on Beckett's Stage

i

Within the vast and varied repertory of late-twentieth-century European drama, Beckett's work would surely be noticed for placing actors in odd, eccentric and otherwise uncompromising stage positions. And that is, as *Footfalls* states things, 'indeed to put it mildly'.[1] Planted in urns or standing stock still on a cold plinth, dumped summarily into trash bins or buried up to the waist, then the neck, in a mound of unforgiving earth – that 'old extinguisher'[2] – the figures in this dramaturgy are more often than not subjected to a highly abbreviated form of physicality, one that demands the *doing* of more and more with less and less, even and especially so in those places where less did not seem possible before. In *That Time*, for example, the actor 'plays' only a disembodied head; and in *Not I*, a *reductio ad hominem*, if not *absurdum*, the lead part is a mouth (as the author said, 'just a moving mouth'), *'rest of face in shadow'*.[3] Little wonder that Jessica Tandy, having starred in the world premiere of *Not I*, decided – and it bears repeating – that she'd 'like to do a musical next'.[4]

Beckett is of course much more than a mere provocateur, although his role as such should not be discounted in the making of such a heady theatrical mix. Yet here the pinpoint precision of his stagecraft has been designed to precede, if not entirely overwhelm, the seductive allure of metaphor and meaning. This playwright can surprise us by revealing his formalist credentials, and most particularly his grounding in theatrical convention, precisely at those moments when the work seems most suspect and most alarmingly avant-garde. What results is a far cry from the sturdy machinery of an Ibsen or a Chekhov, but it is not quite Robert Wilson or Pina Bausch either. Beckett's scenography looks both backward and forward at the same time, celebrating his theatrical inheritance in the very process of transforming it, a method that involves stripping his seemingly minimalist sets of every extraneous detail *plus one*.[5]

Nowhere is this technique more evident than in the uncanny use Beckett makes of the seated figure on stage. The performance history here is huge. Strindberg's *Ghost Sonata* is only one of many plays that revel in the dramatic potential of restricted and limited mobility, though in Beckett's case this particular cross-reference can be illuminating. The image of the Old Man confined to a wheelchair had a profound effect on him when, on Suzanne Dumesnil's urging, he saw Roger Blin's 1949 production on the left bank in Paris, at the Gaîté Montparnasse – an interpretation the playwright later said was true to both 'the letter and the spirit' of the drama[6] (*Endgame*, 1957, was only eight years away). Tennessee Williams exploits the same theatrical trope in the highly atmospheric *Suddenly Last Summer*, although his female incarnation of the device, the gothic horror that is Mrs Venable, appears on stage to inhabit the full force of a sexually charged *drame bourgeois*. Beckett, like O'Neill before him, eschews any such holding of 'the old family Kodak up to ill-nature',[7] and will pursue the seated figure for very different purposes and effects. The western theatrical canon gave him a great deal to choose from.

Shakespeare's seated figures, those that are scripted, are most often discovered in public places: banquet scenes, throne rooms and senate chambers abound. The emphasis would appear to be on spectacle rather than intimacy. As early as *Titus Andronicus*, two noble families who have not previously consumed what remains of one another are prepared to go at it again, seated as they are, fatally, at this last of all suppers. And in a much later drama the irony cuts deep: Macbeth reminds Banquo not to 'fail' his feast. A famous ghost obliges. The large interior spaces where characters are likely to sit in *King Lear*, *Hamlet* or *King Richard III* are also ceremonial, just as they are when they turn legalistic in *Othello* or jury-rigged in *The Merchant of Venice*. Yet Shakespeare's hyperactive heroes rarely sit for long, reluctant as they are to forfeit their empowering vertical positions. No director would allow his stunned Macbeth to remain calmly seated when a ghost materialises on stage so sensationally; nor could the actress playing Lady Macbeth – no 'little chuck' she – resist the opportunity to assert her control over the scene by the simple act of *rising*, as though the text itself were telling her what to do. 'Sit, worthy friends,' she urges Rosse and Lennox and the other nobles gathered at her table. 'My lord is often thus.' Later in the same scene a newly confident Macbeth attempts to reclaim his authority over his wife in much the same way: 'I am a man again. Pray you *sit* still'[8] (emphasis mine). All of this may be nothing, of course, compared to *King Lear*, where the Duke of Cornwall demands that a chair be brought on stage for the blinding of Gloucester. The captive Earl, his hands bound, is in most modern productions thrown backwards as Cornwall plugs his heels into the 'vile jelly'. And then he does it again – because, according to Regan, 'one eye will mock the other' – before this seated figure, as sightless as Milton's Samson Agonistes at Gaza, is returned to an upright position. Only then is Gloucester set free to 'smell his way' to Dover.

Kings, too, may willingly and literally abandon their thrones when the dramatic occasion encourages them to do so: think of Claudius delivering his highly polished speech before the assembled courtiers as the second scene begins in *Hamlet*, or Lear pointing to the redrawn map of the peaceful kingdom he plans to divide among three troubled sisters. And just what is Horatio supposed to do with Hamlet's body at the end of the play when, for this protagonist at least, 'the rest is silence'? Chairs, especially ornamental ones, come in handy.

It might be difficult to appreciate Beckett's fascination with the seated figure on stage without a glance at his ardour for Racine, the subject of a series of lectures he gave at Trinity College, Dublin, soon after his return from Paris as *lecture d'anglais* at the École Normale Supérieure. (Beckett quickly abandoned his academic career because, as he said at the time, 'I could no longer bear the absurdity of teaching to others what I did not fully understand myself.') In plays such as *Phèdre* and *Bérénice* haunting female figures are always suspended on stage halfway between the statue and the statuesque as Racine allows his gorgeous alexandrines to do all the work. But when physical action occurs on this platform it is always arresting. Phèdre never sits. When the seated confidante who is also her alter ego demands to know the details of the dramatic situation soon to unfold, she cries out: 'You want to know what's going on? Stand up!' (translation mine).

Writing in the second half of the nineteenth century for the quite different dimensions of a box set, Ibsen had the opportunity to explore the potential of the seated figure in an entirely new perspective, one that allowed for a far more focused display of psychological texturing. Shaw was quite right in his observation that modern drama began when Nora sat her husband down in the final act of *A Doll's House* to discuss the nature of their marriage.[9] Ibsen is terrific at this sort of thing, efficiently arranging the scenic space to accommodate his characters' need to communicate their innermost thoughts and emotions (it's his substitute for the no-no of soliloquy, realism's bête noire). Nora sits on a love-seat with Mrs Linde, her could-be confidante, first communicating too little, then in a subsequent scene perhaps revealing too much. The same tableau works for her encounter with Dr Rank; she flirts, then recoils from the clumsy declaration that follows. Movement constitutes meaning here, and how the furniture is used speaks volumes. Nora re-establishes the boundaries of their relationship when she turns away, abandons the love-seat and stands, rigid, elsewhere.

The same blocking on the same sort of settee accumulates additional resonances when Ibsen further explores its dynamics in *Hedda Gabler*. Eilert Lovborg joins Hedda on the drawing-room sofa as she invites him to do so, on the pretence of sharing her honeymoon photographs. The tension is palpable; intimate glance and innermost gaze make the most of it. Much of what happens next lies in everything that is *not* said, except for Lovborg's trenchant murmur, 'Hedda Gabler . . .', married name conspicuously omitted. The predatory Judge Brack, a Hedda Gabler in drag, insinuates his presence at her side, too, and on the same divan, at first appearing to have greater success in penetrating the shell she has so elaborately constructed around herself. 'I never jump,' she confides, though she may be forced to do so, and soon, under the threat, albeit unstated, of blackmail. 'Life is not tragic,' Ibsen wrote in the notebook he kept about this play and its lead character's motivation, 'Life is absurd – And that is what I cannot bear.'[10] Defeated, but also a little triumphant, this female figure removes herself from the set and the set-up, sits down at the piano and shoots herself. Brack, startled, thrown off-guard, even shocked into recognition, falls into an armchair, prostrated, and delivers the play's refrain which also serves as its bitter curtain line: 'But good God! People don't *do* such things!'[11] He's right: people don't, but dramatic characters do.

Chekhov, Ibsen's near-contemporary, seems to have been equally astute in recognising the enormous range of possibility for the seated figure on stage. One could even argue that sitting is what Chekhov's characters do best. *Uncle Vanya* opens on a quiet scene like so many others in his *oeuvre* – Astrov sitting and chatting with the old Nurse, but really talking to himself. Vanya awakes from his nap and soon joins him in the garden, as do other members of the cast. They drink tea and in one case perhaps a drop of vodka. Yelena passes by with the Professor, 'too indolent to move'.[12] Scenes from a country life – in four acts, no less – indeed. Yet not every

Chekhov set-to is quite so laid back. The provincial tranquillity has been deceptive. Bedlam will erupt following a busy afternoon of revelatory tête-à-têtes. Serebryakov, the family members gathered all around him, announces a bizarre plan to sell the estate, invest in securities and purchase a small villa in Finland. Vanya, his chronic lassitude for once upstaged, runs into the house to look for a gun. It misfires. 'I missed!' he cries out in dismay and despair (this is, among other things, hilarious), 'I missed twice!' The curtain falls on Act Three before he has a chance to sit back down.

There's so much going on in the first act of *Three Sisters*. Amidst the preparations for the big event marking Irina's name day, with Olga transfixed in monologue – remembering and inventing – we can easily forget that the third sister, Masha, is sitting there in full view, reading, detached and bored. She whistles, then gets up to leave, but not before Vershinin, recently arrived from Moscow, makes a gallant entry into the Prozorov sitting room. 'I'll stay . . . for lunch,' she says, tellingly, joining 'the lovesick major' at the table and foreshadowing everything that will take place between them as time in this drama runs its steady course.

Another Chekhov play, *The Seagull*, even borrows a famous theatrical device from *Hamlet*. Arkadina and Trigorin, not exactly 'guilty creatures sitting at a play',[13] take their assigned places as part of the makeshift audience for Konstantin's literally dumb show, in which poor Nina is forced to play the underwritten lead. 'There are no real people in your work,' she tells the crestfallen young author, who yearns so much to be a writer. As in Shakespeare, the scene, both the play and the play-within-the-play, devolves into chaos, with everyone soon on their feet. Chekhov's drama ends, by contrast, on a more sombre note, and with a greater density of dramatic overtones. With characters concentrated around a card table, a fateful game of lotto is in progress. But so is something else. 'Get Irina out of here somehow,' Dorn tells Trigorin, leading him downstage and away from his seat at the table. 'Konstantin just shot himself.' *Curtain.*

Beckett is by no means the only beneficiary of such a rich and all-inclusive theatrical vocabulary. Playwrights of his generation, as well as those before and after, have embraced the same legacy, re-tooling and refining it in a series of strategies for 'making it new' and discovering their own voices. Caryl Churchill updates the ban-quet scene in her feminist drama, *Top Girls*; Edward Albee care-fully choreographs Peter and Jerry on a fateful Central Park bench in *The Zoo Story*; Sam Shepard finds a surprising locus for a benched father figure in *Fool for Love*; and Harold Pinter, in a cycle of remarkable plays that runs the gamut from *The Hothouse* and *The Birthday Party* to *Old Times* and the 'icy and silent' *No Man's Land*, invests his sedentary characters with blood-curdling, almost demonic, power. 'If you take the glass,' the seated Ruth taunts Lenny in *The Homecoming*, 'I'll take you.'[14] Through a glass darkly indeed; passive aggression like this may never have been quite so dramatically potent before. Less successful, perhaps, is Arthur Miller's attempt to use the image to explore the multidimensionality of paralysis, physical, psychological and political, in *Broken Glass*. What distin-guishes Beckett from his peers, however, is that his solution to the problem is not only practical from a theatrical point of view, but simultaneously analytical. It involves nothing less than a reconsid-eration of how this device might be used within the entire dramatic enterprise itself.

ii

One of the things that makes Beckett an exceptional figure in the development of modern drama is his ability to think outside the box – and especially outside of the box set, the theatre space he was familiar with and the one he was generally writing for. Beckett said he turned to the stage as an escape from the 'awful prose' he was writing at the time. 'I needed a habitable space,' he reflected, 'and I found it on the stage.'[15] But this was also a licence to look else-where for the foundation and formulation of his image-making.

His longtime interest in landscape painting and the representation of interior spaces on a canvas[16] – light emanating from a source outside the frame (as in Caravaggio and Vermeer) – would have enormous repercussions as he quickly adapted such values to the demands of the stage. Yet it is perhaps in the portrait of the seated figure in its many variations, from Raphael to Rembrandt to Van Gogh and contemporary painters such as Francis Bacon and Louis le Brocquy (or Picasso for that matter – think of the long road he travels from the forward-leaning 'Gertrude Stein' of 1905–06 to the cubist conundrum of the 1939 'Dora Maar in an Armchair'), where Beckett finds a grammar and an idiom that he can truly call his own. This is less a question of such one-to-one correspondences as we might be able to locate between a provincial Chekhov scene and the evocative landscapes of his good friend, the Russian painter Isaac Levitan (or between Munch, say, and the late Ibsen), as it is an appraisal of the specific ways in which form gives latitude to meaning.

As early as those gold-leafed Madonnas in Giotto, Cimabue and Duccio, seated as they are so serenely on their earthly or celestial thrones, we already sense the profound mystery of inwardness and the dislocation caused by private thought – not yet 'a voice dripping in [the head]' of the sort Beckett will pursue in *Endgame*, but certainly pointing us in that direction. And such magnificent Marias, flat and elongated though they may be (their chairs come off a whole lot better), are already equipped with distinct personalities. In the embrace of single-point perspective that follows, the characterological basis of such figures will be defined even further in a steady preoccupation with three-dimensionality, sometimes in the fullness of looking out, sometimes through the pensive mediation of searching even deeper within. The seated figure, painted, repainted and represented yet again, was well on its way towards becoming the *sine qua non* of that endless and elusive drama known as human consciousness.

Such implications were not lost by the cautious playwright who became in the 1950s Samuel Beckett. '*In a dressing gown, a stiff toque on his head, a large blood-stained handkerchief over his face, a whistle hanging from his neck, a rug over his knees, thick socks on his feet*', the blinded Hamm, '*in an armchair on castors*' – a gender-bending Madonna on wheels – would seem to epitomise the playwright's fascination with the seated figure on stage.[17] Never neglecting 'the little things in life', *Endgame* allows us to study the image in redacted form: a brief tableau punctuates the mime Clov performs in the drama's opening moments, while it is still '*covered with an old sheet*'. But it is really in the earlier *Waiting for Godot* where this stylisation can be seen to be most firmly rooted. Pozzo even goes so far as to make a fetish of this recurring motif:

> But how am I to sit down now, without affectation, now
> that I have risen? Without appearing to – how shall I say –
> without appearing to falter.[18]

Pozzo, like his author, recognises a good thing when he has it going, and a few minutes later, eyeing the stool, he seizes the opportunity to advance its richly performative momentum:

> **Pozzo** I'd very much like to sit down, but I don't know how to go about it.
> **Estragon** Could I be of any help?
> **Pozzo** If you asked me perhaps.
> **Estragon** What?
> **Pozzo** If you asked me to sit down.
> **Estragon** Would that help?
> **Pozzo** I fancy so.
> **Estragon** Here we go. Be seated, Sir, I beg you.
> **Pozzo** No, no, I wouldn't think of it! (*Pause. Aside.*) Ask me again.

Estragon Come, come, take a seat I beseech you, you'll get pneumonia.

Pozzo You really think so?

Estragon Why it's absolutely certain.

Pozzo No doubt you are right. (*He sits down.*) Done it again! (*Pause.*) Thank you, dear fellow.

In *Godot*, however, the seated figure is assigned a much more primary role than this, and a far more vital one: nothing less than the opening image of the play itself. As the curtain rises (the playwright was certainly thinking of one), we first meet Estragon '*sitting on a low mound*' trying to take off his boot and failing to do so, followed by the quintessential Beckett line, 'Nothing to be done.'

Without calling undue attention to itself, the insistent figure of a man sitting by himself on a stone, Gogo's initial situation in *Waiting for Godot*, has a long provenance in the Beckett repertory. As a semblance of isolation, cosmic and otherwise, it appears not only in the short story 'The Calmative' but also in the second movement of *Stirrings Still*. Beckett seems to have derived this image from the Middle High German poet he much admired, Walther von der Vogelweide, although this is the first time he uses it, albeit ironised, in a play:

> I sat upon a stone,
> Leg over leg was thrown,
> Upon my knee an elbow rested
> And in my open hand was nested
> My chin and half my cheek.
>
> My thoughts were dark and bleak:
> I wondered how a man should live,
> To this no answer could I give.[19]

'Ich saz uf eime steine,' Walther's self-description in the first line of the medieval lyric, inspired the well-known painting of him in the Manesse manuscript; the poet is said to be buried in the cathedral at Würzburg, where Malone recalls having seen 'Tiepolo's ceiling' ('What a tourist I must have been, I even remember the diaeresis, if it is one').[20]

Sitting – and waiting – is Hamm's celebrated 'speciality' in *Endgame*, although Beckett's tramps already exploit most of the latter's potential in *Godot*. Thinking on his feet to pass the time that would have passed anyway, but 'not so fast', Vladimir in fact rarely sits down, but he will do so, and poignantly, on those few occasions when he tenderly comforts his partner. Poor Lucky, of course, is never permitted the same luxury, even though 'he carries like a pig' and falls down in an ever-maddening sequence of verticals and horizontals, culminating in a dance variously called 'The Hard Stool' and, more significantly, 'The Net'. Much comes together for Beckett, however, in the work that explores the dark underside of *Godot*; and it will be *Endgame*, as 'dark as ink',[21] that finally allows him to write his own signature on the seated figure stranded on a lonely set: 'Outside of here it's death.'

iii

Even as a student at Trinity, Beckett saw Belacqua, the Florentine lute-maker who appears early in his fiction by way of Dante (and who re-emerges in various guises throughout the prose writings), as the seated figure par excellence. In *Purgatory* his role is both tantalising and suggestive. Chided for his negligence, he responds with the words Aristotle assigns to him, and which provide Beckett with the title of a short story published in 1932: *Sedendo et quiescendo anima efficitur sapiens*. The Poet's riposte in *The Divine Comedy* could not be more stinging: 'Certainly, if to be seated is wise, then no one can be wiser than you.'[22] In his prose fiction Beckett transforms such habitual laziness and such exquisite verbal sparring – for that is what it is – into his own version of some dematerialised 'Belacqua bliss'.[23] But in theatre indolence has to be animated; there's sitting, and then there's sitting squared.

For the actor playing Hamm, planted so magisterially on his own throne, *Endgame* can be daunting in just how much it asks him to act, to do and to perform.[24] Sloth does not enter into the equation. Clov, who has 'work to do' and cannot sit down, is a whole lot more than stage manager, caretaker or mere retainer here; he's also the engineer for rapid transportation as he wheels his master from place to place around the circumscribed 'world' of this interior set, placing him, one more time, smack 'in the centre' – or thereabouts. Hamm, too, is called upon to play any number of roles: he is (or has been) at various times a storyteller, a master jokester, a consumer of sugar-plums, a dispenser of biscuits and pap, a vengeful son, a drug user, a sentimentalist, a tyrant, a dog lover and an enviable appreciator of technical stage terminology. He may also be a father. *Endgame* requires a remarkable series of gestures from this seated figure in order to develop a complete character and take full charge of the stage.

Oddly enough, *Krapp's Last Tape*, a work for only one player, presents a view of the seated figure that offers the audience both more and less. Krapp seems at first reluctant to play this part. Jangling keys, uncorking a bottle or retrieving a dusty old dictionary, he shuffles back and forth into the darkness of the set before settling down into the dimness that grudgingly illuminates his small table. Preparatory rituals completed, the 'play', so to speak, is now ready to begin for this 'wearish' figure, face mostly forward as he confronts that perilous point where time remembered becomes the consciousness of time remaining. The past, transformed on tape, alternately startles and plagues him with its steadfastness, and it is his misbegotten 'vision' that even at this late date still tampers with it. 'Play' as it will be defined on this platform therefore involves mostly playback, this one from the resources of memory stored in 'box three . . . spool five'.[25] Reaction constitutes the action here –

so much so that the actor must carefully calibrate his every move to accommodate the dictates of Beckett's multifaceted and highly literary script. Face and upper body are of crucial importance in *Krapp's Last Tape*, for, as light fades downward, it obscures all that might otherwise be revealed.

On tape the recorded voice of Krapp – at thirty-nine – says he will 'feel' a black ball in his grip until his 'dying day', a cue for the most nuanced of hand gestures. And when, after a pregnant pause, the voice from the same past comments on the 'new light' above the desk as 'a great improvement', weary eyes seemingly veer upward. As noted in the case of *Macbeth*, this text, too, goes a long way in stimulating the seated figure's animation. But not every suggestion of movement in this drama will evoke a similarly kinetic response, however discreet it may be meant to be. Some can only be taken at *face value*: the image of the lovers together on a punt before ardour compels a much younger Krapp to lie 'down across her', his 'face in her breasts' and his 'hand on her', or the more recent and quite different memory Krapp records in the present, that time he went to Vespers 'once', fell asleep and rolled off a pew.

In a fourth major play, *Happy Days*, Beckett emerges once again as 'a great leg-puller and an enemy of obviousness'.[26] Winnie's physical situation, planted as she is in the earth, the playwright's update of some Mesolithic burial site from the Boyne Valley due north of Dublin (the scale more reminiscent of Loughcrew than Newgrange or Knowth), will be difficult to determine. It is hard to tell – 'imagine' really, as Mouth says in *Not I* – 'what position she is in', 'whether standing or seating or kneeling' (in production, the solution is best left to the techies). Seated behind the mound, and barely within our sightline, is the ever-patient Willie – 'ever', that is, until the play's stunningly ambiguous conclusion. And it is the blocking for this enigmatic figure that will be of most interest to us here. In the first act Winnie 'sits', to speak strictly metaphorically 'in the old style', in the privileged position; for it is she – and she alone – who can twist her neck back in order to receive a better view of this less-than-demure seated male figure. As she shifts her observational position for greater visibility, we must take her word for it when she reports that he picks his nose, looks at porno-graphic postcards or spreads sunscreen over the various parts of his body best left unmentioned. By contrast, we can just about see a snippet from the local newspaper when Willie turns a page to read from the obituaries: 'His Grace and Most Reverend Father in God Dr Carolus Hunter dead in a tub.' Winnie reacts to this alarming news with an exclamatory 'Charlie Hunter!' in what the script calls a '*tone of fervent reminiscence*'.

Two short works first produced in 1981, *Rockaby* and *Ohio Impromptu*, as well as the earlier *Come and Go* (written in 1965), offer us compelling variations of the same motif. These are highly compressed dramas that start with a specific image, ignite a com-plex emotion, then open up a universe of feelings and ideas.[27] You enter this theatre feeling fairly secure of your intellectual bearings, but leave less certain, curious – and challenged. 'When did we three last meet?'[28] Vi recites at the opening of *Come and Go*, inverting a line of inquiry previously assigned to one of the three 'weird sisters' in Shakespeare's *Macbeth*. Vi sits at the centre, side by side with Flo and Ru as Beckett's three female figures are stationed stage right, motionless and very erect, facing front, hands clasped in laps. Each gets up, turn and turn about, then returns to the place of origin, re-inscribing the initial static tableau, isolated and illuminated as it is by a single ingot of unforgiving light. 'Does she not know?' / 'Does she not realise?' is this text's ominous take on the old vaude-ville game of who's-on-first; but in this case the consequences, unstated though everywhere implied, are likely to turn lethal. Closure is achieved when the seated figures are arranged somewhat differently, but only just so: resuming the positions in which they were first discovered, they now have their hands clasped, resting on three laps to signal end of play. Flo delivers the curtain line, 'I can feel the rings', followed by the palpable silence that finally engulfs them all.

Rockaby is similarly attuned to the mysterious, even mystical quality of inwardness that portraitists have often found so seductive in the features assigned to their own seated figures. Beckett recycles the rocking chair from his novel *Murphy*, but in the play he elevates its status to that of a character in its own right. A 'prematurely old' female figure sits 'subdued' in *Rockaby* on a chair that is 'controlled mechanically', without her assistance. The playwright was clear about one thing: the Voice of memory, recorded, initiates the rock, not the other way around, and certainly not the woman dressed in black who yearns to hear so much 'More'.[29] Beckett preserves the enigma as well as the integrity of this dramatic moment by insisting on 'the absolute absence of the Absolute',[30] relying instead on the image and the modesty of its scale to insinuate presence through a fusion of light, sound and movement rather than narration. His dialogue is poetic, not surprisingly so in this case, as it is there to complement and elevate the stage's searing visual lyricism. Rarely has a seated figure on stage, 'mother rocker' notwithstanding, been asked to carry the weight of so many competing discourses, one in which theatre technology wears such a disarming human face. 'La Berceuse', the title Van Gogh gives to his well-known portrait of the seated Mme Augustin Roulin (*Berceuse* is also the title Beckett uses for the French translation of his play), is therefore much more than a cross-reference or a convenient painterly analogue. French *berceuse,* moreover, means cradle, lullaby *and* rocking chair; but it can also refer, as it does in Van Gogh, to the seated figure herself. Beckett's drama in performance will be, experientially, all of these things at once.

The affective nature of such formal restraint achieves additional resonance in *Ohio Impromptu*, where the figures seated at a plain deal table are both singular and doubled: *'As alike in appearance as possible.'*[31] Reader and Listener are each other's Other; and each is each other's '*Hypocrite lecteur, – mon semblable, – mon frère!*' (see Baudelaire).[32] Perilously, as in Dante, '*Simile qui con simile è sepolto*', like with like is buried here.[33] But are we really seeing double, or merely some liminal fantasy of a replication hysteria, an uptake of the riveting stage dynamics called for by Goldoni in *I due gemelli veneziani*? Or are Beckett's spellbinding seated figures only two aspects of one man – for, inevitably, as you read you also in some sense profoundly listen? Stage left one figure intones the cherished lines from an old volume, monopolising the soundscape and complicating its strangeness with the suggestion of narrative. Stage right the other 'other' carefully weighs every word; his 'knock' is opened wide when it signals an unexpectedly sudden interruption to the couple's tacit interaction, only to magnify it further when L compels R to retrace his steps. Only the re-reading counts, as Nabokov said.[34] Then, when we least expect it, stage imagery is quietly redrawn as the seated figures achieve unprecedented momentum. The 'story', such as it is, being done, the seated Reader very slowly and very deliberately closes the book on us:

> *Knock.*
> *Silence. Five seconds.*
> *Simultaneously they lower their right hands to the table, raise*
> *their heads and look at each other. Unblinking. Expressionless.*
> *Ten seconds.*
> *Fade out.*

iv

While Beckett's work for the mechanical media might be best discussed in another forum, it could be argued here that his depiction of the seated figure is offered much greater amplitude and precision in the plays written for television. Subject to sharp definition by the camera lens, the images we see delineated in complex pieces like *Eh Joe*, *Ghost Trio* and *Nacht und Träume*, as in Beckett's 'comic and unreal' *Film*, come to us both scrupulously edited and pre-recorded, like fleshly eruptions in an otherwise spectral world. But that is their limitation as well as their considerable strength – the fact that they are frozen, so to speak, in time and on magnetic tape. The illusion of spontaneity and of spontaneous gesture, so crucial to the impact of Beckett's seated bodies in live performance, as when Reader and Listener synchronise their movement at the conclusion of *Ohio Impromptu,* or when the actress suddenly utters 'Fuck life' seemingly out of nowhere just before she bows her head in *Rockaby*, empowers such figures to command the space they inhabit with emphasis and authority. What may be lost in exactitude is made up for in fineness; and as the light slowly fades on the set for each play, it provides the theatre audience with another kind of permanence: a fixed after-image that lingers in our imagination forever.

Beckett's stage, as this examination of his innovative use of the seated figure attempts to show, is always full of 'high-class nuts to crack'.[35] But that is not to say that the solutions he finds so appealing are without precedent. Beckett draws upon a rich vocabulary of theatrical convention, analyses his inheritance, then takes it several steps forward. The hardest nut to crack for Beckett, as for Shakespeare, Ibsen, Chekhov and so many other playwrights before him, will always be found, after all, in that delirious and probably delusional seeing-place he knows and we know as 'theatre'. *See better. Fail better.* Followed in his case by that agonising – but also inspirational – one word, 'On.' What Beckett so impressively adds to this ongoing discussion of the seated figure on stage is how he seems to know from the start that in theatre, as in life, you're sometimes a lot better off 'on your arse than on your feet'.

CHAPTER 6

Beckett's Devious Interventions, or Fun with Cube Roots

i

Playwrights sometimes have an odd way of insinuating their presence in the scripts they provide for theatrical realisation, a collaborative process at best.[1] In the modern European repertory Pirandello could get a laugh, and then a laugh laughing at the laugh, by having his much put-upon Director in *Six Characters in Search of an Author* demoralise his cast by denigrating, then demonising, the metaphysical flights of fancy composed by a well-known Sicilian writer from Agrigento, a code-cracker who just happens to be called Luigi Pirandello. Brecht similarly acknowledges himself in one of his several ideas for staging *Mother Courage*; one can even imagine an alienation device near the end of the play when Anna Fierling steps out of character to announce to the audience that 'Mr Brecht' now requires her to sing a hymn of mourning over the dead body of her daughter Kattrin.[2] Shakespeare himself was not above such self-referencing, although he does so more covertly, as when he has Prospero famously valorise 'the great globe itself', his own company's performance space, elsewhere recorded as the 'wooden O' and 'this majestical roof fretted with golden fire'.[3] Beckett, a close reader of dramatic texts like these, offers such works the highest form of compliment – imitation – when in his early, uneven play *Eleutheria* we hear about a mysterious 'Mr Beckett', some sort of (possibly) Irish Jew of dubious connections who, like Mr Godot himself, never appears on stage.[4]

Now this is something quite different from what we mean when we say that a drama is Chekhovian or Pinteresque or Brechtian or, for that matter, Beckettian. Terms like these, bound to be descriptive rather than analytical, want to communicate something affective and generally positive about tonal qualities, hard-to-quantify stage realities such as sensibility, atmosphere and mood. They can even be useful in helping us to understand and appreciate more fully the art and craft of playwriting itself, questions of form and style and, above all, of dramatic technique and the skillful manipulation of theatrical convention. How often do we say we 'hear' the voice of Ibsen trumpeting the clarion call of real as opposed to surface and official morality beneath the psychological quandaries of the sad figures he presents in *Rosmersholm*, *Ghosts*, *Little Eyolf*, *The Lady from the Sea* or *Pillars of Society*? His American heir, Arthur Miller, just barely avoids the tipping point of lecturing us through his own moral compass when he 'speaks' to us with so much certainty and assurance in compelling works like *All My Sons*, *Incident at Vichy* and, most persuasively so, in *The Crucible*.

Shaw always does this, and not only in his discursive prefaces; he was essentially writing drama to get his audience round to his way of thinking. His transformative but not always appealing ingénues like Ellie Dunn, Barbara Undershaft, Vivie Warren and even Saint Joan are there to remind us of the challenges he faced in always being right. Less doctrinaire, dramatically speaking, Sartre, Camus and Genet similarly make their presence 'felt' in masterful works such as *Huis Clos*, *Caligula* and more conspicuously so in the final speech that brings down the curtain in *Le Balcon*.

Chekhov complicates matters with his deceptive pose of object-ivity, the good doctor witnessing from afar the foibles of an ensemble of disaffected Russians stranded seemingly without hope on a provincial estate that has seen better days. The axe is about to fall; no more cherry orchards. At best, his characters will have to settle for a smaller place, perhaps only a villa in Finland. The Chekhov script was supposed to offer his audience, as in his *Uncle Vanya*, merely discrete 'Scenes from Country Life in Four Acts'. To his brother Mikhail he confided that when writing he liked to keep in mind the metaphor of a courtroom, as though he were passively seated there as a juror observing a real-life drama, at times even a melodrama, unfolding before his very eyes.[5] Well might we ask along with Beckett's Gogo, 'Who believes him?' Didi's response is very much to the point: 'It's the only version they know.'[6] Chekhov's presence, it could be argued – his wit, his irony, and above all his compassion – is there in almost every line of dialogue he wrote for his actors, and not only those in which they start talking to pieces of furniture. Beckett might say (and in fact did say) that 'it's all a question of voices, no other image is appropriate'.[7] But how and when and why the 'voice' of a playwright emerges to make itself heard within the material limitations of a given performance space will make all the difference in the dynamics of representation that is an integral part of each and every staged world.

ii

As we might expect, a master playwright like Beckett goes about all of this quite boldly and very differently. In the drama he writes, his signature is palpable and real – and we sense this, as in Chekhov, almost everywhere. It is, moreover, 'something' the author himself seems to have been aware of, as when he characterised the late play *That Time* as 'something out of Beckett'.[8] Given such pervasiveness, an element of Beckett's dramaturgy more fundamental than a wink or a nod, the signature's legibility can be, however, surprisingly difficult to decipher. In this chapter I would like to suggest a number of ways Beckett relies on a series of devious interventions to make his authorial presence known when each one of his staged dramas takes on its highly determined 'course'.[9]

Let us begin with a detour. In *All That Fall*, the radio play Beckett wrote in 1956, broadcast a year later on the BBC, his unregenerate walk-talkers are nothing if not fully wired for verbal pyrotechnics. And none more so that Maddy Rooney, née Dunne, 'the big pale blur' who makes use of a highly arcane and archaic vocabulary despite her assertion to the contrary: 'I use none but the simplest words, I hope, and yet I sometimes find my way of speaking very . . . bizarre.'[10] One would have to look at Oscar Wilde's Lady Bracknell – or the young Lady-Bracknell-in-training who is her daughter Gwendolen – to find a rhythm and a rhetoric to match the rodomontade of this kind of speechifying: 'What kind of a country is this where a woman can't weep her heart out on the highways and byways without being tormented by retired bill-brokers!' 'Christ – what a planet!' – indeed. 'This is worse than the Matterhorn.' Nobody talks like this, even in Ireland (although from time to time you might hear something like 'I'm coming, Mrs Rooney. I'm coming, give me time, I'm as stiff as yourself / Stiff! Well I like that! And me heaving all over back and front. (*To herself.*) The dry old reprobate!'). Nobody, that is, except actors and that other Trinity College playwright, Oscar Wilde. In *The Importance of Being Earnest* all of the players sound exactly like him. And while this is by no means true of Beckett in his first play for radio, one can't escape the impression that he, too, keeps 'feeding' his characters lines that are, strictly speaking, out of character – more *trompe l'oreille* than *trompe l'œil*.

'Well,' says the dark Miss Fitt, worried about the fresh lemon sole for lunch and the delay entailed in offering Mrs Rooney a 'helping hand' up a steep staircase to the railway platform, 'I suppose it is the *Protestant* thing to do' (emphasis mine). A tight-fisted and fierce Anglican, Hetty, whom Maddy dubs that 'Fitt woman', can be very 'distray', even as a churchgoer; when the sexton passes around the plate – 'or bag, whatever it is they use' – for the collection, she remains stern and unmoved, alone as she is 'with her Maker', 'oblivious to [her] co-religionists'. Mr Slocum – his is another ticket name – uses another kind of Beckett talk when he responds to Mrs Rooney's question about what in the world he thinks he's doing not coming directly to her aid as he sits high up in his automobile with its new balloon tyres, 'Gazing straight before me' through the windscreen, as he says, 'into the void.'

Mrs Rooney can be similarly outspoken. When she encounters a familiar cyclist on the dusty country road, a normally timid man is soon left cursing 'God and man . . . and the wet Saturday afternoon of [his] conception'. Not to be outdone, she suddenly cries, 'It is suicide to be abroad. But what is it to be at home, Mr Tyler, what is it to be at home? A lingering dissolution.' Later in the play's verbal action Dan Rooney goes so far as to wonder aloud about every word his wife employs, including the penchant for phrase-making we've heard before – 'cleg-tormented eyes', 'all this ram-dam' and 'quivering like a blanc-mange' are three of her choicest selections from an ever-expansive Beckett lexicon of eccentric terms – and the even more peculiar manner of her on-air delivery: 'Do you know, Maddy, sometimes one would think you were struggling with a dead language.' And you know all at once that you are overhearing Beckett when you listen to a character apostrophising an undergarment: 'O cursed corset! If I could let it out, without indecent exposure.' Is Maddy even aware that she's paraphrasing Shakespeare in a wild parody of *Hamlet* ('O cursed spite / That I was ever born to set it right!')? In his early fiction Beckett was always worried about giveaway lines like these. He despaired in his novel *Murphy*, published in England in 1938, that all the characters 'whinge' sooner or later, with the possible exception of the title hero, 'who is not a puppet'. 'It was clumsily done,' the young writer observed with acute self-perception, some embarrassment and considerable dismay. 'You could see the ventriloquist.'[11]

In writing stage dialogue for the two major plays composed during the same general period as *All That Fall* – *Endgame* and *Waiting for Godot* – Beckett struggles hard to liberate himself from the perils of what he once characterised as 'soliloquy under dictation'.[12] And in these works he mostly succeeds. *Godot* depends on the sharp distinctions the playwright makes between one famous stage figure and another, and those distinctions are physical as well as verbal. Body language here can speak volumes, as Gogo and Didi each walk a different 'walk' and each talk a different 'talk', Pozzo and Lucky in the first act even more so. They even play their silences differently. So just where does Beckett 'come in' here, if not exactly on his 'hands and knees'?

Puppet-master that he is, Beckett can assign words to characters whose meaning has an uncanny and unsuspected way of eluding them, just as their provenance is something of which they are at best only dimly aware. Didi's 'caryatids', which he employs not quite accurately – now just where did that come from? – is a case in point, as is Pozzo's impossible-to-pin-down 'knook'. ('*Knook*,' the playwright demurred. 'A word invented by me.')[13] Does Gogo, the tramp who claims to have once been a poet, know that he is quoting from both W.B. Yeats and *The Gospel according to St Matthew* when in all innocence he tosses off a weighty lyrical line like 'The wind in the reeds'?[14] A formidable if equally suspect ally in intertextuality, the more circumspect Didi is assigned a series of lines reflecting his more philosophical inclinations. Yet here, too, the playwright may be showing his hand; when the critic Vivian Mercier complained that he sometimes made his characters 'sound as though they have PhDs', Beckett's calculated response was both self-conscious and evasive: 'How do you know they hadn't?'[15]

And moving on from the possibly sublime to the eminently ridiculous, what are we to make of the dog who appears in the kitchen to steal a loaf of bread in Didi's sorry song that opens the play's second act? One does not wish to ruin the *rundegedichte*, but the eyes of dogs, even those who come running, don't read, though they will do so, miraculously, in this work's musical interlude, *pace* Beckett. So, too, is the confusion of names straight out of this playwright's personal vaudeville prompt book: Pozzo? Bozzo? 'I once knew a family name Gozzo. The mother had the clap.' Beckett can be seen to be even more intrusive in this landmark work when he breaks the frame of the sturdy proscenium, sending Vladimir scurrying offstage for a pee (prostate trouble), and reminding the audience once again that they are not only watching a play, but, Pirandello-like, a play written by Samuel Beckett.

iii

In the hermetic world of *Endgame* such stylisation on Beckett's part can be far more difficult to track and trace, but it is there all the same; and its pinpointing can be writ large in the drama's irresistible theatricality. What, Hamm queries Clov early on in the first published edition of the play, 'No telephone calls?' And all those metatheatrical elements built into *Endgame*'s crisp, efficient and deceptively simple dialogue – Hamm's reliance on 'an aside', a 'soliloquy' and a 'subplot', not to mention his self-conscious deployment of the word 'dialogue' itself – are the same sort of 'magnifier[s]' Clov will use when he turns the lens of his telescope on the audience to acknowledge their presence as well as the author's: 'I see a multitude in transports of joy.'

Such virtuosity – for that is what it is – will be extended and developed even further in *Krapp's Last Tape* and *Happy Days*, where the intrusion can be both comic and strategically potent from a dramatic point of view.[16] In the first of these two major works, a duet for one player (Beckett wrote the piece for the great Irish actor Patrick Magee), the author insinuates his presence from the very beginning when he situates us in Krapp's den '*A late evening in the future*'. Tape recorders were new to Beckett at the time he composed this one-act play (1958), a consequence of his attempt to listen to *All That Fall* on the tape shipped to him from London on a machine he had recently purchased for this purpose in Paris. To account for Krapp's voice captured electronically on 'box three, spool five' made some thirty years before, with its trenchant commentary on a tape made even earlier, Beckett, who never forgets 'the little things in life', sets the stark presence of his drama in a dark time still to come: 'Just been listening to an old year,' the voice intones on tape, 'passages at random. I did not check in the book, but it must be at least ten or twelve years ago.' Krapp's balletic fumblings with this machine, winding its spool back and forth until he locates a much-longed-for romantic passage with the girl in the punt, is of course a sharp reminder of the profound emotional effects Beckett can wrest from the deft manipulation of mechanical media, an aspect of his work that will be explored with much greater finesse in the later plays for radio, and even more so in his highly sophisticated work for television. Within the dialogue of *Krapp's Last Tape*, Beckett is 'there' with us too, and all the way, most especially so with his introduction of the prop of an over-size dictionary. His player consults this dusty old book to look up the word *viduity* he no longer understands:

> State – or condition – of being – or remaining – a widow – or widower. (*Looks up. Puzzled.*) Being – or remaining? . . . (*Pause. He peers again at dictionary. Reading.*) 'Deep weeds of viduity.' . . . Also of an animal, especially a bird . . . the vidua or weaver bird . . . Black plumage of male . . . (*He looks up. With relish.*) The vidua bird!

The playwright lets the resonances fall where they may.

Krapp's Last Tape features a number of other Beckettian overtures. Foremost among these is of course the 'memorable equinox' that can no longer be remembered, as well as the retreat from the sublime to the ridiculous in what can only be described as the strange affair of the black ball: 'Her moments . . . my moments . . . the dog's moments.'

Even churchgoing is subject to something resembling authorial parenthesis: 'Went to Vespers once, like when I was in short trousers . . . Went to sleep and fell off the pew.' And when the curtain rises on a female figure buried up to her waist in a mound of earth in the opening moments of the next play, *Happy Days*, you know for sure that the self-same 'Mr Beckett' is there to greet you once more with still another display of 'laughing wild amidst severest woe' (if you miss the point, he will be there for you again at the opening of the much shorter Act Two, where we discover Winnie now buried up to her neck). The vocabulary the intrepid Winnie uses to pass the time of day in this drama's 'blazing' light seems to be coming from the same prompt book that by this time in the repertory is beginning to sound both *outré* and agonisingly familiar: I refer you to words like 'formication' (with a medial *m*) and the stage business involving 'hog's setae' (hilariously, Winnie asks what a hog is, exactly, not *setae*, leaving most of us, Latinists excluded, in the dark).

'An organised mess', this character is also a mouthpiece for what her author long ago disparaged as 'the loutishness of learning'[17]. She remembers, although her author allows her only to half-remember, bits and pieces from what might have been in 'the old style' a vast array of cultural patrimony. This she carelessly mangles, then re-mangles, in a series of terrific one-liners derived from the mightiest of mighty literary sources – for example and among others, Thomas Gray, Robert Browning, Shakespeare, Verlaine, Aristotle, Samuel Johnson, Dante, Yeats, the Psalms and Proverbs – and even early Beckett. 'What are those wonderful lines?' is a lament that quickly becomes her melodic refrain, theme and broken variation notwithstanding. How has Winnie, a not 'too capable woman' and 'a bird with oil on its feathers',[18] acquired such a hefty, albeit fractured, frame of reference? Is she quoting from failing memory, off-book, so to speak, and did she ever really get these lines straight? I wonder. The irony in her impressive citation of the Miltonic 'Hail, holy light', which she uses to open the play's second act, is, like so much else in her richly intercalated wordplay, a gift the playwright lavishes on his audience, not on his lady-in-perpetual-waiting, '*blond for preference*'.[19] And in this respect 'The Waltz Duet' from

The Merry Widow, which she hums as the author closes his play, may be the bitterest pill of all. Although Winnie can be counted on 'to put a bit of jizz into it', Beckett may be playing his character, once again, like a violin. Sometimes the joke's on her, especially at those moments when her comments are 'a bit off colour', as she might indeed say. 'Don't curl up on me,' she encourages her man, pre-Viagra style, 'I may need you later.' At full stretch – pun intended – how better might this author 'glorify the Almighty' than by laughing with *us* at *his* jokes, particularly 'the poorer ones'?

iv

It should come as no real surprise that in the later, short plays, the intricate works that follow *Happy Days* (*Oh les beaux jours*), what I'm calling Beckett's devious interventions should stand out in much sharper relief.[20] Within these minimalist thresholds any deviation matters, especially those that disrupt a stage atmosphere previously established. In *Play*, a piece written soon after *Happy Days*, his characters, one male adulterer and his two women, are potted and plotted in funereal urns, '*Faces so lost to age and aspect as to seem almost part of urns.*' And in this less-than-elegant *drame bourgeois*, a French farce sited in some circle of Dante's hell, the farcical elements are not where one would normally expect to find them. All this is, of course, 'just play', as the dialogue reminds us, but a 'play' in purgatory – if that is indeed where we are. Sufferers in eternity, however, are unlikely to hiccup, as they do here.

A sharp, conspiratorial spotlight awakens the figures, turn and turn about, from darkness and silence, allowing them to speak their self-indulgent piece; but the spotlight can also shut them down, bored with the predictable triangularities of their thwarted love-knots, invariably ho-hum. W2, the proverbial 'other woman', fears that 'things may disimprove, there is that danger', while W1, the woman scorned and done wrong, shouts 'Get off me!', threatens to cut her throat, then thinks better of it and hires a 'first-rate' man to 'dog' the competition instead. The whole charade 'stink[s] of bitch'. But the voice of the playwright can be heard coming through most clearly in a line he assigns to M, his jaunty fornicator: 'Personally, I always preferred Lipton's.' 'Adulterers, take warning, never admit.'

In the plays written in the 1970s and 1980s – works that objectify the subjective ordeal of diminishing bodies that harbour immortal longings – the tone is far more sombre, just as the rhythm, the pacing and the language is more haunting and elegiac. But that is not to say that Beckett's devious interventions have come to a sudden end. Indeed, as the examples I cite next hope to illustrate, they appear in odd corners of the drama more startling and more vigorous perhaps than ever before. *Footfalls*, the play Beckett wrote for Billie Whitelaw,[21] is a case in point. The language here is profoundly lyrical, although it is nowhere monotone. The drama is a dialogue, really, and one that is discretely, though sparingly, divided into several unequal, semi-autonomous parts: first May and the voice of her mother speak, then Voice alone, then May alone, before silence has the final say. Beckett has obviously learned a great deal from his exploration of radio drama, where 'the sound of a human voice' has the ability 'to evoke an entire world'.[22] And the 'tangle of tatters' that constitutes the stark image of a pacing May, 'faint' and 'pale grey', although 'by no means invisible, in a certain light', is the perfect visual analogue to everything we hear, words and chimes combined: 'Watch how feat she wheels.'

One would hardly expect to find any disruption on a playwright's part to break the extraordinary mood of visual drama and the sense of scale so unerringly established here, but, suddenly, there it is in the intervening story of an 'old Mrs Winter, whom the reader will remember' (and I am not referring to the amen-stuck-in-his-throat lifted so slyly from Shakespeare's *Macbeth*[23]). Note in this case how a literally spectacular voice – a voice-over in point of fact – now imposes itself on the dialogue-within-the-monologue:

Old Mrs Winter, whom the reader will remember, old Mrs
Winter, one late autumn Sunday evening, on sitting down
to supper with her daughter after worship, after a few half-
hearted mouthfuls laid down her knife and fork and bowed
her head. What is it, Mother, said the daughter, a most
strange girl, though scarcely a girl any more . . . (*Brokenly.*)
. . . dreadfully un– . . .

How does a 'reader' – Beckett's reader? – negotiate his or her
uneasy presence into the pacing of this particular drama? Who,
indeed, is this 'old Mrs Winter', and just where, exactly, is she to
be found? Surely no one has been able to locate her within the
wide scope of Beckett's repertory. So, well might we ask, where has
all of this 'this' come from, if not from that self-same 'Mr Beckett',
once more insinuating his presence into the drama that suddenly
unfolds. More disingenuously, perhaps, we hear his intrusive voice
elsewhere and again in the very same play: 'When other girls of her
age were out at . . . lacrosse,' the Voice intones, 'she was already
here.' Beckett said that his critics (this one included) were going to
have a field day with this one – and he was right.[24]

He was also right about the first-night audience's reaction to
Ohio Impromptu. He told Stan Gontarski, to whom he delivered
the script as a likely showpiece for the 1981 academic conference
organised at Ohio State University in Columbus, that when the
curtain rose on his two identically dressed and wigged figures
seated at a plain deal table, the audience would laugh.[25] They did.
Reader and Listener (actor and audience) represented the seminal
figures of so many other Beckett displays, just as the pun on *nuits
blanches* – 'White knights now again his portion' – signalled the
site of the Beckett Archive at the Whiteknights campus in Reading.
The academically inclined might also be able to appreciate the reference to the Isle of Swans, the place on the Seine where the playwright went on his Paris walks with Joyce: 'Stay where we were once

so long alone together, my shade will comfort you.'[26] More sly, perhaps, is Beckett's sudden insertion of yet another 'authorial' intrusion, Reader's ambiguous reference to the 'redoubled force' of 'the fearful symptoms described at length page forty paragraph four'.

In *Rockaby*, performed the same year in Buffalo, New York in relation to another symposium, this one arranged by Danny Labeille,[27] biographical details like this are more deeply embedded in the text, if they can be said to exist at all. The first of Beckett's dramas to be written specifically in verse, and one that from the opening note of 'More', followed by *'Pause',* then *'Rock and voice together',* appears out of the dark to foster a retrospective mood seemingly immune to any exterior alteration. A woman in a chair, 'prematurely old' and dressed in black, with light concentrated on face, unkempt hair and huge eyes, is more than enough to establish this play's highly evocative tableau, where even the most subtle of gestures is infused with meaning and dramatic power. 'Ah yes, we've been here before,' observed Billie Whitelaw, who initiated the role in Alan Schneider's premiere production.[28] And as the recorded voice runs its course and the synchronised movement continues, the piece as a whole seems determined to maintain the lineaments of its persuasive interior landscape. 'Till in the end', at close of play, when 'Fuck life' ungraciously intrudes. Mother-rocker notwithstanding, even in this bleak 'close of a long day' – 'rock her off / rock her off' – Beckett reminds his audience that he is there still, orchestrating his drama's 'more' spectacular emotional effects. Perhaps the Director in *Catastrophe* is speaking for him, too, when he laments 'this craze for explicitation! Every i dotted to death!' A few lines later in the same torture chamber the fur-clad impresario may speak to his female Assistant, surprisingly this time, in the playwright's political voice: 'What next? Raise his head? Where do you think we are? In Patagonia?'

In his very moving television play from 1976, . . . *but the clouds* . . ., broadcast on the BBC as part of a programme called 'Shades',

Beckett's roll-over technique can be observed in subtler but even more consequential terms. A homage to Yeats,[29] whose great poem 'The Tower' provides the playwright with his title (and much more), the piece allows us to envision with an isolated male figure the fading memory of a lost one as the beloved's scrim-like face uncannily makes itself telegenic in three separate guises: (1) she appeared, and 'in the same breath was gone'; (2) she appeared and 'lingered', with 'those unseeing eyes I so begged when alive to look at me'; and (3) she appeared, and 'after a moment' lip-syncs the concluding stanza of Yeats's poem, which the male figure's pre-recorded voice intones in slow, poignant relay. There is of course a fourth case, 'by far the commonest, in the proportion say of nine hundred and ninety-nine to one, or nine hundred and ninety-eight to two'. And this is precisely where Beckett walks straight into his drama. In this 'case nought' the erstwhile lover begs in vain, late into the night, but no apparition greets him. He waits until he wearies, then ceases his night-time vigil, busying himself 'with something else, more . . . rewarding, such as . . . such as . . . cube roots, for example, or with nothing', 'busying himself with nothing, that MINE . . . ' In-between such pregnant ellipses we hear Beckett speak, 'I pray you,' and he speaks, as he has so often done before (only this time electronically) 'trippingly on the tongue'.[30]

V

What are we to make, finally, of so many devious interventions on the part of this playwright's complicated art and craft, working, as we might expect, overtime? It might be far too easy to dismiss this as one more example of Beckett's obsessive control over his place in the theatre, as though his many interpreters, actors, directors and designers alike, were merely there to service him in the lead role. But I think that this is not really the case here. Artists have a long history in the western tradition of writing their signatures into their work, and they sometimes do so in oddly provocative ways, most pointedly so in the Italian Renaissance, a moment of classical revival, revisionism and adaptation that Beckett knew only too well – so much so that he could evaluate a given artist's formal virtuosity as well as his flaws with determination, even zeal.[31] Raphael paints himself into his famous 'School of Athens', as does Benozzo Gozzoli in his beautiful procession of the Magi kings in the Palazzo Medici-Riccardi in Florence, the same city where Andrea del Sarto also makes his appearance known in his bold designs for the forecourt of the Annunziata. Poor Tommaso, too, dead at twenty-six, better known as Masaccio, frescoes himself into a probable self-portrait in the Brancacci Chapel at S. Maria del Carmine, as does Filippo Lippi in his pictorial cycle of St Stephen and John the Baptist in nearby Prato.

More profoundly, perhaps, Michelangelo intrudes his presence as a signature in the 'Dies Irae' of 'The Last Judgment' in the Sistine Chapel, and later sculpts himself as the rueful old Nicodemus in his great unfinished 'Pietà'. And only recently at the Uffizi restorers discovered – uncovered really – Caravaggio himself lurking in his famous rendition of 'Bacchus': in the jug to the right of this famous epicene figure the artist painted the silhouette of a person standing with one arm stretched forward and with clearly distinguished facial features, especially the nose and eye (we can now also see the collar). This is very likely Caravaggio's self-portrait, reflected in the pitcher before him as he was painting.

Impersonality, much vaunted by grand modernist writers such as T.S. Eliot, now seems very much beside the point (Eliot was for Beckett, as he wrote in an early letter, only 'TOILET spelled backwards').[32] The devious interventions that bring so much regenerative spark to the narrative dimensions of Beckett's drama are there, so to speak, to lighten the load, and to remind us once again that although there is loss, a bang and a whimper, there is also the far more difficult challenge of just going on. Irony, but humour too, runs deep in what the intrepid Winnie would surely call 'those wonderful lines', dialogue encounters that dazzle, then strike us on further reflection with their author's pervasive presence: 'The creatures, the creatures,' Hamm obliges in *Endgame*. 'Everything has to be explained to them.' Nell, not to be outdone, is gifted an opening line so outrageous – but so adventurous, too – that one can almost hear its author howling away somewhere in the distance: 'What is it my pet, time for love?'

'Like the look of him?' the Assistant wonders in rehearsal about the high-value detainee standing before us on a bone-chilling plinth in *Catastrophe*. Tonight we (all but) improvise.[33] Beckett's tyrannical Director seems pleased with this arrangement: 'Terrific. He'll have them on their feet. I can hear it from here.'

CHAPTER 7

Beckett's (What?) Romanticism

i

Beckett's early confrontations with a profound romantic impulse, surprising for an artist whose popular reputation rests on the rapture of nothingness and the embrace of the existential void, are the centre of considerable disruption and unease; and, as we might suspect in a writer with 'an itch to make',[1] they display the adamancy of a beginner. There's an awful lot of textual anxiety. Here parody, though clearly a mask, serves him well. Not for the young author of 'Walking Out', one of the short stories published in *More Pricks than Kicks,* the tempting delusions of 'The Lake Isle of Innisfree' by 'the Nobel Yeats';[2] even in the 1938 *Murphy,* far 'less Wordsworthy', escape means 'chaos' and 'superfine chaos' means 'gas'.[3] Strategic diversions like this will continue even in the trilogy, and most notably in *Molloy,* where Gaber/Youdi's flamboyant colonisation of 'life' as 'a thing of beauty and a joy forever' is the vain subject of comic deflation, although piercing all the same: 'Do you think he meant human life?'[4]

Such a corrupt figuration of 'Endymion', turned on its head as noted earlier, is not, however, necessarily absolute; something – a part – of the youthful Keatsian reverie remains. That 'trace', too long ignored according to C.J. Ackerley and S.E. Gontarski, is beginning to show signs of remarkable resilience. And as Philip Laubach-Kiani argues, that romantic discourse is very much a part of what makes 'Beckett the [quintessential] European'. Beckett wrote to Thomas McGreevy as early as 1930:

I like that crouching brooding quality in Keats – squatting
on the moss, crushing a petal, licking his lips and rubbing
his hands, 'counting the last oozings, hours by hours'. I like
him best of them all, because he doesn't beat his fists on the
table. I like that awful sweetness and thick soft damp green
richness. And weariness. 'Take into the air my quiet breath.'

Yet how Beckett liberates himself from parody to confront the
romanticism inherent in his own 'profounds of mind' is a story of
artistic maturity still waiting to be told.[5]

Beckett's fiction might seem at first glance an odd place to look
for this sort of transformation. Yet even in the pre-trilogy fiction,
it depends very much on where one is looking and what one is
looking for. The brashly overwritten *Dream of Fair to Middling
Women*, always on the verge of being toppled by the sheer weight
of its allusive name-dropping ('I vow I will get over J.J. [James
Joyce] ere I die. Yessir.'),[6] and the relatively more austere *More
Pricks than Kicks* that follows, appear to have left any trace of romanticism at least one century behind. *Murphy*, too, has its broken-
down heart located elsewhere: it's hard to find transcendence in
scenes set in West Brompton or the lavatory of the Irish Abbey
Theatre, Oscar Wilde notwithstanding. ('We are all in the gutter,'
Alma quotes him in Tennessee Williams's *Summer and Smoke*, 'but
some of us are looking at the stars.') *Watt,* the novel Beckett wrote
in Roussillon in the south of France when he was hiding out from
the Nazis, is another matter altogether. This four-part invention,
part Faulkner, part New Testament, turns narrative certainty on its
head; its central figure, the 'long wet dream with the hat and bags',[7]
is on a futile journey to find nothing less than 'home'. Postmodern
nostalgia is surely one way to account for this. But even Beckett's
nuances have nuances: *isn't it* [sort of] *romantic?* Molloy's quest
may be similarly motivated and similarly imperilled; only in his
case he ends up in a ditch.

Beckett's fierce trilogy – *Molloy, Malone Dies* and *The Unnamable* – is determined, however, to take us elsewhere. Part of the intrigue of this fascinating enterprise lies in the way Beckett's storytellers work overtime (and over time) to find an authentic narrative voice – and he, that is Beckett, along with them. Even more than a half-century after its composition, it's still difficult for anyone seriously concerned with writing not to be impressed by the trilogy's monumental achievement. Considerations of form, not the least of which is the very form of the novel itself, become part of the breathless storytelling: in the beginning, as in the anxious middle and the richly symphonic end, is, as it always already was, *the word.* 'You must go on, I can't go on, I'll go on' – the long-awaited *terminus ad quem* of *The Unnamable*[8] – celebrates nothing so much as itself: language, so to speak, given viable material flesh. Such romanticisation of the word, and what it can be made to do on its busy journey to nowhere *in particular*, in this sense rivals Ulysses 1 (Virgil by way of Homer) and *Ulysses* 2 (Joyce); it might even make us think even more so of the heady triumphalism in 'Ulysses' 3 (Tennyson): 'to strive, to seek, to find, and not to yield.'[9]

Tim Parks is quite right when he says that throughout Beckett's writing, despite the pyrotechnics, and most especially so in the trilogy, 'We come across passages of haunting descriptive power in which we cannot help feeling the author has a considerable emotional investment.'[10] *What tenderness in these little words, what savagery.*[11] That emotional pull will take on a surprising romantic complexion in a second trilogy that begins with the composition of *Company*. In this eloquent work non-linearity is made linear as the malleability of time, as in Chekhov, is as much a character as any other. Past and present frame each other; and each literally contextualises the other. A voice comes to one in the dark, to one, moreover, on his back in the dark; and as it does so it gathers up fragments of memory with a force so strong that it seems that almost everything else might be annihilated.

Such determination to recapture the past, and to lyricise it this time so confidently in prose, demonstrates just how far Beckett's fiction has travelled from the posturing of its early beginnings. In this regard the trilogy that begins with *Molloy* and ends with *The Unnamable* serves a mediating function as a sort of clearing-house for narrative bric-a-brac, 'a little yes, a little no, enough to exterminate a regiment of dragoons'.[12]

It offers us, of course, many other things as well, including the opportunity to see how a moment from the past is shaped into words that will be before long reconfigured and reimagined in *Company*:

> One day we were walking along the road, up a hill of extra-
> ordinary steepness, near home I imagine; my memory is
> full of steep hills, I get them confused. The sky is further
> away than you think, is it not, mama? It was without malice.
> I was simply thinking of all the leagues that separated me
> from it. She replied, to me her son, It is precisely as far
> away as it appears to be. She was right. But at the time
> I was aghast. I can still see the spot, opposite Tyler's gate.
> A market-gardener, he had only one eye and wore side-
> whiskers.[13]

The highly evocative passage from *Malone Dies* is quickly con-taminated when a very different rhetoric uneasily and abruptly intrudes: 'That's the idea, rattle on,' as though the text needed to remind itself that it better not go too far in this direction. The beast, however, isn't quite so easily tamed; for in Malone's very next line, 'You could see the sea, the islands, the headlands, the isth-muses, the coast stretching away to north and south and the crooked moles of the harbour.' Embarrassed, perhaps, this self-censor tries again:

> My mother? Perhaps it was just another story, told me by
> someone who found it funny. The stories I was told, at one
> time! And all funny, not one not funny. In any case here
> I am back in the shit.[14]

By the time Beckett's mature fiction revisits the same moment
some two decades later in *Company*, intercalations like this one
have been carefully erased. More secure in itself, the voice no
longer needs or desires self-pity or self-laceration. What emerges in
the process is a kind of ultimate liberation, a freedom to encounter
the past without shying away from any or all of its romantic
implications. The child is the father of man, *tout court*. And the
text, reinvented, now speaks 'voice verbatim',[15] all gimmicks gone:

> You make ground in silence hand in hand through the
> warm still summer air. It is late afternoon and after some
> hundred paces the sun appears above the crest of the rise.
> Looking up at the blue sky and then at your mother's face
> you break the silence asking her if it is not in reality much
> more distant than it appears. The sky that is. The blue sky.
> Receiving no answer you mentally reframe your question
> and some hundred paces later look up at her face again and
> ask her if it does not appear much less distant than in reality
> it is. For some reason you could never fathom this question
> must have angered her exceedingly. For she shook off your
> little hand and made you a cutting retort you have never
> forgotten.[16]

Close readers of *Company* will be sure to notice how Beckett gives
an easy rhythm to the voice of memory and a far more circumspect
one to the voice of reason, then lets the two play off one another
in vigorous counterpoint. That second voice, always commenting
chorus-like, despite 'the state of faint uncertainty', edits and revises

itself as it too goes along, playing its assigned part as 'Devised deviser devising it all for company.'[17] The voice of memory, on the other hand, displays no such hesitation and no such trepidation:

> You stand on the tip of the high board. High above the sea.
> In it your father's upturned face. Upturned to you. You
> look down to the loved trusted face. He calls to you to
> jump. He calls. Be a brave boy. The red round face. The
> thick moustache. The greying hair. The swell sways it
> under and sways it up again. The far call again. Be a brave
> boy. Many eyes upon you. From the water and from the
> bathing place.[18]

Yet readers of Beckett's late fiction should not necessarily assume that the same elements on display in *Company* are the ones to be found with a similar level of coordination in the works that follow. Beckett's romanticism, if it exists there at all, is in every instance nothing if not case specific. *Ill Seen Ill Said* and *Worstward Ho* are poised, moreover, in very different directions, and romantic elements will be far more difficult to certify as such. The former, for example, configures a highly suggestive and mysterious moonlit landscape in which the individual remains isolated before the vastness of a cold and uncomprehending universe, as though the pathetic fallacy were rendered this time as truly pathetic. And though this might be read as a *Wuthering Heights* redux, a hundred thousand years later, nature itself, while not quite dead, appears both unresponsive and indifferent to 'the farrago from eye to mind'.[19] The piece is by no means 'abstract', but rather what its author once called a 'metaphysical concrete': 'object not exploited to illustrate an idea . . . The communication exhausted by the optical experience that is its motive and content.' The situation is even more bleak in the ninety-seven paragraphs that comprise *Worstward Ho*, 'Said nohow on.' Here there is no meaning, at least none that can be found in an easily defined way; significance, yes – affects, authority, mystery, all singular and all unchanging. 'A pox on void.'[20]

ii

Beckett's romanticism follows a very different trajectory in the theatre when, in *Krapp's Last Tape*, a machine invades his stage geography and the same romantic texture can be viewed from a slightly different angle; and this time, once again, the 'angle' is no longer one of 'immunity'.[21] Still reluctant to give up on parody, even at times farce – this old drunk goes to Vespers and falls off a pew; he tells Fanny, that 'bony old ghost of a whore', that he'd 'been saving up for her' all his life – Beckett's 'Magee Monologue' nevertheless presupposes a world where nature, for one, has not necessarily 'forgotten us'. Consider, for a moment, the play's most lyrical passage, the one this study has noted before where Krapp valorises and memorialises his encounter with the girl in the punt, a picture that never, ever fades into nothingness, just like Keats's 'thing of beauty'.[22] The passage, its words, its images, its sounds, reach for their true voice of feeling as we, like Krapp, revisit them through a deliberate process of cyclical repetition:

> . . . I said again I thought it was hopeless and no good
> going on, and she agreed, without opening her eyes. (*Pause.*)
> I asked her to look at me and after a few moments –
> (*pause*) – after a few moments she did, but the eyes just
> slits, because of the glare. I bent over her to get them in the
> shadow and they opened. (*Pause. Low.*) Let me in. (*Pause*).
> We drifted in among the flags and stuck. The way they
> went down, sighing before the stem! (*Pause.*) I lay down
> across her with my face in her breasts and my hand on her.
> We lay there without moving. But under us all moved, and
> moved us, gently, up and down, and from side to side.[23]

Now just where, exactly, did that come from? Certainly not from the same place where the thirty-nine-year-old Krapp we hear on the same tape concocted his pretentious Byronic 'vision': that formulaic 'crest of the wave' takes place in a dark landscape replete with 'great granite rocks', 'the foam flying up', and is illuminated by the perilous beam of a faraway 'lighthouse' – not surprisingly, the most heroically romantic of isolated architectural structures. So much 'storm' and so much manufactured stress: 'All Sturm and no Drang.' The image is – how shall I put it? – a bit tired and, on Beckett's part, deliberately composed to sound trite, a sure recipe for any author's *not* 'getting known'. No wonder Krapp has sold so few books.

James Knowlson, Beckett's most reliable biographer, has none-theless linked Krapp's 'vision at last' to the author's own moment of awareness, one that took place in his mother's room during one of his periodic visits to his family in Ireland.[24] Yet, however much this incident satisfies a need to 'historicise' Beckett's recognition that 'darkness' would become the true inspiration for his work, such information tells us very little about what actually happens in the play, where that 'moment' is transferred to the ferry wharf at Dun Laoghaire. When Krapp listens to himself on the tape he made almost thirty years before, almost as though the past was pausing on its way towards oblivion, his attitude is anything but honorific; and Beckett, moreover, is not Krapp.

Defying time, but soon undone by it, Krapp keeps winding his tape back, and back again, to the lyrical passage on the punt quoted at some length above. He approaches this set piece almost as he might another character; and Beckett allows him to do so in a profoundly reverential manner. Through the will and force of his own subjectivity, Krapp yearns to be in silent dialogue with it again, to hear from it once more, and then again once more. As do we, the members of this play's captive audience. Each time the act of listening, both Krapp's but ours as well, is effectively called into question.[25] Frozen, so to speak, on magnetic recording tape (despite my questionable metaphor), the lines are always the same; yet as the tape winds backwards, then forwards, then backwards once again, we hear them as different ('We know it by heart,' as a later text will have it, 'and yet the pang is ever new'[26]). Such secure placement and *replacement* and *displacement* in the text – these lines will prepare us, too, for the play's closure – guarantee their privileged position in the emerging soundscape, making us conscious of the work's heartbreaking rhythm of return.

Certainly the image of a love long lost is one of the more familiar tropes of heterosexual, male-centred romantic fantasy; only in death can the female figure live fully. Yeats, in particular, can be spectacular on this point, as Beckett well knew when he relied on 'The Tower' for the controlling metaphor he used with so much dramatic authority in . . . *but the clouds* . . . . Here's Yeats:

> Does the imagination dwell the most
> Upon a woman won or a woman lost?
> If on the lost, admit you turned aside
> From a great labyrinth out of pride,
> Cowardice, some silly over-subtle thought
> Or anything called conscience once;
> And that if memory recur, the sun's
> Under eclipse and the day blotted out.[27]

Krapp's 'woman lost', like Yeats's, never stood much of a chance anyway, reduced as she is in both cases to mythic figuration, objectification and perhaps even invention – one more 'dark lady', one more 'belle dame sans merci', one more Mona Lisa smile (in Beckett's . . . *but the clouds* . . . she's reduced to a mere scrim). Her image is, nonetheless, all that 'remains of all [Krapp's] misery': 'A girl in a shabby green coat, on a railway-station platform.' Well, and something else too, perhaps, despite the narcissism and the arrogant masculinist egocentricity: the ingenuity and genuine grandeur of haunting lines that finally put to rest what has been shown to be in performance a truly compelling drama.

> Here I end this reel. Box – (*pause*) – three, spool – (*pause*) – five. (*Pause.*) Perhaps my best years are gone. When there was a chance of happiness. But I wouldn't want them back. Not with the fire in me now. No, I wouldn't want them back.

> *Krapp motionless staring before him. The tape runs on in silence.*

Why does this ending work as forcefully on us as it does? Perhaps because in this play Krapp, the so-called hero, is its self-inflicted victim; he is also an ambiguous figure who sits apart from the action, thinking about it. Isolated and alone, and with the requisite hint of dementia vying with moments of heartrending lucidity, he is sometimes grandly stoical, at other moments far less so. Forcing himself to remember, to remember – to memorialise and re-imagine a past which can be brought back only in and by words – he is simultaneously wistful and forgetful. And in this troubled and wilful blurring of time present and time past, his participation in the drama, oddly enough, is anything but tentative.

Beckett's deliberate staging of a man with a recording machine allows him to exploit the rich dynamics of a highly efficient framing device. Crude by today's supremacist standards of electronic intervention (even the cassettes Beckett later uses in his television play *Ghost Trio* are now horribly out of date), Krapp's bulky tape-recorder is nonetheless an effective instrument for keeping romanticism in check. The machine, clumsy player that it is, is also the stage prop that ironises and particularises it. Without its inspired intrusions, its nerve-wrenching switching on and off, its cruel and fateful mid-sentence rewindings – grinding away so harshly at 'lies like truth'[28] – even the erotic evocation of the girl on the punt might be rendered as agonisingly absurd. For by the time Beckett comes along his late-modernist audience is no longer willing to take such 'splendour in the grass' at face value.[29] Beckett finds in Krapp's machine, awkward though it may be, the potential to give technology a human face – and a tender one at that – where we may have least expected to find it. And as he does so he discovers his principal means to re-channel and reposition a romantic impulse that is anything but sentimental.

That is making yet another large claim for Beckett, but the proof of it will come in the late, great works he designed for the stage and the mechanical media. In complex dramas like *That Time*, *Footfalls* and *Rockaby*, Beckett displays just how much he has learned about 'the sound of the human voice' and 'its power to evoke an entire world'.[30] He did so before, in the radio play *All That Fall*, but it is not until *Krapp's Last Tape* that the recorded voice and the seated figure of the actor on stage develop such a convincing *pas de deux*. Part of the affective nature of this elegant duet depends on the coordination of technology with live stage action, without which dramatic tension cannot occur.

In the plays for television which date from the same general period, that tension and that conflict will become even more vigorous and precise. Working with expert technicians like Jim Lewis, first at the BBC and later at Süddeutscher Rundfunk (SDR),[31] Beckett showed himself to be a sensitive collaborator, especially when questions of rhythm, harmony, colour (or its conspicuous absence), atmosphere, the structure of the piece and the spirit of the piece demanded a heightened sense of the camera's vulnerability to the effects of recorded sound with light, movement and meaning. What emerges, especially in highly lyricised pieces like *Nacht und Träume*, . . . *but the clouds* . . . and *Ghost Trio*, is nothing less than the evocation of intensely realised romantic images, all the more compelling because of their technological discipline and proficiency. Nor is that steady reliance on (in this case) televisual machinery absent from the eye and ear of the viewer: 'Mine is a faint voice. Kindly tune accordingly . . . Having seen that specimen of floor you have seen,' rectangularly, 'it all.'[32]

Much of what I am trying to argue in this chapter will depend, as we might expect, on the instance of performance, how directors and especially actors respond to Beckett and to Beckett's intrusive but intuitive romanticism. 'Play the line' is a mantra always worth repeating when staging such complicated texts; but what to do with that line when it has, at times, a decidedly romantic edge? How it works and why it works – and *if* it works – will only come through in the theatre. Those competing moments of pathos (or is it simultaneously bathos?) – for instance, box three, spool five's 'her moments . . . my moments . . . the dog's moments' – only serve to render that romantic impulse ever more cauterising, as Krapp-at-sixty-nine, 'all to end', discovers to his peril. This 'is what we call making an exit'.[33]

Beckett actors have responded to this challenge differently: Patrick Magee, for whom the piece was written, with a baritone of verbal nuance; a burly Jack MacGowran with sweaty determination; the great Canadian player Donald Davies with enviable understanding of the work's opposing moods and alternating inflections; a thin, pale, gaunt and frail-seeming John Hurt, by holding the illusion of vexed interiority confronting the tragedy of failing memory on a darkened stage; Hume Cronyn by allowing silence to have its persuasive say; and finally Pierre Chabert, who appreciated the rich pun on the play's French title, *La Dernière bande*, by emphasising the translation's other *double entendres*. (I omit Giancarlo Canteruccio's 1996 rendering of *L'ultimo nastro di Krapp* featuring two desks and two Krapps at the Teatro Krypton in Scandicci, but share with the reader my confusion by citing Malone's response to Sucky Moll's earrings: 'Why two

Christs?' implying that one was more than enough – besides, as 'the reader will remember', Christ was in her mouth).[34]

Beckett's romanticism may be, as these strong actors might be among the first to appreciate, just a lot of crap; but it also means a very great deal for the drama that develops for his Krapp with a very big 'K': that seedy old figure of a drunk whose tense inter-actions with magnetic recording tape have the potential to disarm us so unexpectedly – so poignantly, too, just as Beckett's fiction has done – in this solo performance event, not so solo and so prosaic after all. In the Beckett canon, as his drama and fiction unfold, they energise and illuminate one another, often in the oddest of places. Those 'traces blurs signs'[35] of a not-always-latent romanti-cism are yet one more way in which they seek so passionately – so convincingly, too – to do so. Thinking about Beckett, you some-times find a new drama in the text in those broken-down corners where you may have least expected to find it.

CHAPTER 8

Beckett's 'Beckett': So Many Words for Silence

> *'Silence is so absolute.'*
> Mark Rothko

i

This chapter begins by urging the reader to observe with its author a full moment of silence, as follows:

. . . .
. . . .
. . . .
. . . .
. . . .
. . . .
. . . .
. . . .
. . . .
. . . .
. . . .
. . . .

'Something,' as Beckett might say – and in fact did say – 'is taking its course.' But what, exactly? *'Silence once broken will never again be whole.'*[1]

Now, any number of things might have happened to interrupt the moment of silence this page has just tried to manufacture. Who knows? You may have laughed, or sighed, or burped, even cried out in dismay. A stomach may have grumbled. That is what live, warm bodies do: throats clear, mouths cough, there's sneezing and – who knows? – perhaps (the matter's delicate) even a Beckettian 'fart fraught with meaning'.[2] A pager may have rung. A beeper might have gone off. A battery in a hearing aid might have suddenly set off an alarm. Then there's the omnipresent cell phone. The clock ticks. A foot taps. A pencil falls to the ground, or a paper clip, a coin, a piece of miscellaneous paper. Is there music in the background? A door slams. Is the American reader chewing gum or – worse still – is 'lip lipping lip'?[3] And so on. Such a busy world! This reading space in which you sit or stand or lie, too, is hardly inviolate: sounds from a hallway and a street life beyond may have already fouled this lame and scripted session of sweet silent thought. Above all, literally, there's the treacherous white noise of electric lights. Proust would be very dismayed. And, to top it off, framing 'it all',[4] there may even be the spectacle of you, reading aloud.

As a celebrated European writer of fiction, poetry and drama (including in this case the plays written for both the live stage and the mechanical media), Beckett is of course well known for the liberties he has taken with such strange texts of silence. He is by no means the first to have done so. The contentious modernist tradition, from Lamartine to Mallarmé, from Proust to Joyce to Pound, from Schoenberg to John Cage and Giorgio Morandi,[5] has been from the start hell-bent on cauterising stillness in word and image and sound: *so* many words for silence, so *many* words for silence. But perhaps more so than any other writer of his generation, Beckett structures an absence that is fraught with consequence, yielding (when it works) a resonant blank, full of gestural vigour and pungency. In his case, the 'earth might be uninhabited', as in *Le Dépeupleur.*

The lone figure in the single-act *Krapp's Last Tape* is only one of many lost ones we will encounter in Beckett's enigmatic repertory of solitary searchers. 'Silence and darkness were all I craved,' cries his simulacrum in *Play*, this time planted – buried really – in an urn. 'Well, I get a certain amount of both. They being one.'[6] 'Now the day is over, / Night is drawing nigh-igh,' intones Krapp as he stares into stage nothingness near the end of his dubious recording session, his performance richly ironising the lines of a Protestant hymn he can barely remember from his long-ago youth: 'Shadows – (*coughing, then almost inaudible*) – of the evening / Steal across the sky.'[7] The rest – and Beckett will show it to be the much greater part – is silence.

An Irish writer of the mid-twentieth century, Beckett inherits a tradition of the half-light, the gloaming, a liminal world that is always on the verge of being recovered in some unspecified else-where halfway between perceived silence and arrested speech – 'relieved', as Didi says in *Waiting for Godot*, but at the same time 'appalled'.[8] His early writings, in English and in prose, like to intellectualise *vacuum* and theorise *plenum*, as though further Celtic twilights, all passion spent, might be put on some indefinite hold, not quite gone but definitely moving in that direction. His novel *Murphy*, published in London by Routledge in 1938, opens with a real 'stinger': 'The sun shone, having no alternative, on the nothing new.' So far so good. But before long the eponymous hero, whose 'fourth highest attribute' is said to be silence, is bound naked to a rocking chair, contemplating in his own time and in his own garret space the dizzying vastness of a 'superfine chaos' most readers would be tempted to call, by contrast, the void:

Now the silence above was a different silence, no longer strangled. The silence not of vacuum, but of plenum . . .[9]

Beckett's imaginative world will not take fire, however, until he agrees to let the silence in, *both* the vacuum *and* the plenum, not making it – whatever 'it' is – into something else, 'the screaming silence', for example, 'of no's knife in yes's wound'.[10] And that's what this critic calls, following Hamm's lead in *Endgame*, a real magnifier:

> Who may tell the tale
> of the old man?
> weigh absence in a scale?
> mete want with a span?
> the sum assess
> of the world's woes?
> nothingness
> in words enclose?[11]

Beckett's cautionary lyric from the Addenda to *Watt*, the novel he was writing in English during the period he was trying to elude the Gestapo by hiding out in the south of France, already thematises the creative dilemma of not-quite-being-there that will shadow Beckett's work over the next four decades. Even earlier than *Watt*, in the famous letter he wrote to his German friend Axel Kaun on 9 July 1937, he begins to speculate on a highly problematic 'literature of the unword' that may finally let silence have its authoritative and persuasive say:

> As we cannot eliminate language all at once, we should at
> least leave nothing undone that might contribute to its
> falling into disrepute. To bore one hole after another in it,
> until what lurks behind it – be it something or nothing –
> begins to seep through; I cannot imagine a higher goal for
> a writer today. Or is literature alone to remain behind in
> the old lazy ways that have so long ago been abandoned
> by music and painting? Is there something paralysingly
> holy in the vicious nature of the word that is not found
> in the elements of the other arts? Is there any reason why
> that terrible materiality of the word surface should not be

capable of being dissolved, like for example the sound
surface, torn by enormous pauses, of Beethoven's seventh
Symphony, so that through whole pages we can perceive
nothing but a path of sounds suspended in giddy heights,
linking unfathomable abysses of silence? An answer is
requested.[12]

Building silence into words will become for Beckett a real 'teaser',
always a question in his 'case nought' of vision rather than technique, although the formidable techniques he develops to do so
will be everywhere immaculate and precise.[13] In these post-
poststructuralist days terms like 'vision' and 'technique' seem to
have fallen on hard times, if not into downright disrepute, but they
are nonetheless the terms Beckett uses to frame Beckett's 'Beckett'.
These are, moreover, the same congratulatory notes he will sound
to negotiate a space for his writing in between a constructed 'said'
and the ever-elusive 'unsaid', then, teasingly, in the even wilder
territory that separates the 'unsaid' from a previously unchartered
'ununsaid'. So much for the 'Art and Con'.[14] Erasure has rarely
been subjected to the firm pressure of such an arch and heavy and
equally deceptive hand. A term like overdetermined now seems
once again like some giddy understatement. The same, of course,
might be said of Dante.[15]

Beckett's maturity as a writer comes with the composition of
Molloy, *Malone Dies* and *The Unnamable*, the three novels he
started writing in French in the late 1940s, then translated fairly
quickly into English (although it did not seem so at the time).
With virtually simultaneous publication on both sides of the
Atlantic, the trilogy, as it became known, soon established his
credentials as *the* fifties writer, the most remarked-upon prac-
titioner of all that was fractious and hilarious and nouveau in the
nouveau roman. In these books Beckett literally writes himself into
the void as his heroes, talkers really, rush pell-mell into silence,

every story's final destination. Molloy ends up in a ditch, while the tables fatally turn on his could-be clone, also known as Jacques Moran, the Frenchified Irishman; Malone dies, or at the very least suffers a cataclysmic novelistic knockout; and what we may have taken for the Unnamable's endless tirade, despite all protests to the contrary, famously stops dead:

> . . . you must go on, I can't go on, you must go on, I'll go on, you must say words, as long as there are any, until they find me, until they say me, strange pain, strange sin, you must go on, perhaps it's done already, perhaps they have said me already, perhaps they have carried me to the threshold of my story, before the door that opens on my story, that would surprise me, if it opens, it will be I, it will be the silence, where I am, I don't know, I'll never know, in the silence you don't know, you must go on, I can't go on, I'll go on.[16]

End stop. So many, many words, only to arrive at silence, which was always already there, waiting for Beckett, at the beginning of his tri-part tale. 'After all,' as Murphy says, after all is said and done and spoken and written down, 'there is nothing like dead silence'. Quite. Murphy's words ring true. The novel has proven to be a clumsy vehicle indeed for letting silence speak its text into this lame unwording of the transparent word. There must be other stratagems.

ii

In the interval between the completion of *Malone Dies* and beginning work on *The Unnamable*, Beckett had the idea of writing a play, mostly, as he told Colin Duckworth, 'as a relaxation, to get away from the awful prose I was writing at the time'. 'I wrote *Godot*,' he noted in 1985, 'to come into the light. I needed a habitable space, and I found it on the stage.'[17] The shift in genre will have enormous practical consequences that bear not so much on the metaphoric representation of silence as on its actual evolution into a highly choreographed performance space. In the theatre Beckett will make silence toe the line. Stage directions like *'pause'*, *'brief tableau'*, and *Waiting for Godot*'s unforgettable *terminus ad quem*, *'They do not move'* will freeze the action, letting silence hold the stage with authority, sometimes even poignancy. Ellipsis, as in Winnie's bravura exploitation of this device in *Happy Days*, allows silence, now palpable and theatrically real, to punctuate, formalise, advance, even dictate the direction of the multiple resonances built through nuance into her richly intercalated monologue.

Here, too, an embedded *pause* will quite literally allow silence to perform itself, reversing our normal expectations for the conventional relationship between text and subtext. Expanding the moment and arresting the action, silence chastens and conditions dialogue until, beaten into something like submission, it reappears in a rhythm of return, tail, so to speak, between its legs. Mime, as in Clov's spectacular 'opener' in *Endgame*, extends the moment even further. Now playing a duet with the lead, silence musicalises Clov's physical action, clarifying and elevating the complicity of movement in the communication of all stage meaning. Silence, *so to speak*, has suddenly upstaged the provenance of the word.

That is not to say that Beckett's trilogy fiction, so far as silence is concerned, is not without its considerable charms. Although the dual struggle to *be* silent and to let silence *be* is always getting caught in its own delirious traps – and particularly memorable are the ones it now deliberately, now inadvertently sets for itself (as in the humdinger, 'I am obliged to speak. I shall never be silent. Never.') – such 'idle talk' is nevertheless heard, as fiction generally is, in silence (unless we assume that this outlaw fiction is designed to be read fully and completely out loud, as the actor Barry McGovern has done, a point to consider later in this chapter). In *Watt* Beckett tried to describe this phenomenon as something like 'a disquieting sound, that of soliloquy, under dictation'.[18] But such a mechanism, clever though it is, will not hold still. The very act of saying 'silence' makes it far from 'absolute', as all three texts in the trilogy are quick to acknowledge. This unnamable subject that both spurns and desires a name sure runs into problems here (*celui-ci*) – as well as there (*celui-là*). The speaker speaking this speech before long finds himself, in spite of himself, narrativising and thematising like crazy. And yet 'the real silence' is supposed to – and for once in a way let's agree to split the infinitive – only and elegantly *be*.

What a lot of words this trilogy will use to talk instead *around* the subject, if indeed there is (only) one. The so-called silence is at various times alleged to be 'little', then 'tiny', then 'unbroken', then 'black', then 'immaculate', then 'grey', then 'perfect', then 'comparative' (there's a good one), then 'outside', then 'inside', then 'long', 'true', 'the same', 'murmurous', 'short', 'absolute', 'profound', 'different', and 'strangled' (my list is not complete).[19] In this ruinous catalogue every word is 'very rightly wrong', both 'ill seen' and 'ill said'.[20] And each is fated to be equally metonymic, for each can only render up a small part of some unobtainable (w)hole. Undaunted, the emerging word-horde (in various places referenced as 'wordshit')[21] holds out the hope of a miraculous 'dream silence' and – get this – a 'silent silence'. Can it be that fiction itself is running out of adjectives – or rather that it 'dare not be silent for long, the whole fabrication might collapse'? The inscripted silence that cannot be described is also 'prohibited'; on the one hand the text is 'condemned to silence', but on the other hand it has a so-said 'right' to it. On 'the brink of silence' there are, suggestively, 'confines of silence', 'drops of silence', 'an instant of silence', 'a second of silence'.

Although 'not one person in a hundred knows how to be silent', *things* – and in Beckett there is nothing like things – will be rumoured to be mysteriously silent: the dust, various objects, the grave, 'my last abode'. 'To restore silence' is in fact 'the role of objects'. At times such equivocal silence can only be captured in metaphor or simile, as in 'the faint sound of aerial surf'. Beckett's narrator 'yelp[s]' against such infelicitous flights of fancy 'in vain', for, as he says, 'that's the worst, to speak of silence'. He longs to 'enter living into silence', but then again he has to admit that there's 'something gone wrong' with it; 'it can never be known'. So many words bring the speaker and this speech (not to mention every reader of the trilogy) 'not a syllable nearer silence'. The fundamentalist taxonomy has been a fraud, a complete waste of time. So, finally, 'to hell with silence'.

But then, again, when and where the reader least expects to find it, 'silence falls with rhetorical intent'. There is at long last at the conclusion of this trilogy the blissful finitude of a signature ellipsis, that silent place where the *what* and the *where* of any fiction must end: '. . . . .'

That is all.
Make sense who may.
I switch off.[22]

iii

Beckett's formalist concern – for that is how it is – with the evocation of silence will get a new lease of life once he turns his attention to the stage – and in ways that may have surprised even himself. For in the theatre Beckett will be free to explore the mediation of *silence*, *pause* and *pacing* as economical and efficient grace notes, attenuated time signatures establishing both movement and meaning. When the poor player struts and frets his hour upon Beckett's stage, as on any other, this certainly can signify a whole lot more than nothing. Let us think for a moment of Shakespeare, always a reliable but problematic repertory when it comes to figuring out just where silence is supposed to fall. Shakespeare's script will be hard to quantify here. But that should not indicate that in performance the text must necessarily surrender itself to a director's sometimes heavy hand.

When, for example (and as Malone says, 'there is nothing like examples'), Othello is about to kill Desdemona in V.ii.7, Shakespeare gives him a curiously suspended line: 'Put out the light, and then put out the light . . . ' What is this line supposed to mean? Punctuation, in this case a marked caesura, calls the reader's attention to a pause that must break the line. What the caesura tells us is that we must not in any case recite the line, staccato, like this: 'Put-out-the-light-and-then-put-out-the-light . . .' In this line the caesura is, among other things, the guarantor of metaphor: without silence there will be no meaning here. As always in textual studies of Shakespeare, meaning determines sound; but from the line's point of view it is really the other way around.[23] Just how long does this silence want itself to *be*? And of course there can be no pause here unless it is surrounded and shaped by the sound of Shakespeare's language, a rich 'farrago' indeed 'of silence and words'.[24]

This 'pell-mell babel of silence and words'[25] presents us in *Macbeth* with still other problems. In this play an even shorter line can speak volumes, as when Lady Macbeth responds to her husband's hesitation at executing the bloody regicide at hand. 'If we should fail?' he cries out at I.vii.59. She completes the broken pentameter line with two well-chosen words: 'We fail?' What roles does silence want to play here in establishing the dynamics of potential meaning in this line? Is it, among other possibilities, *We? Fail?*, or is it, rather, the upended shrug of *We fail!* Caesura will not be of the slightest use to us in this instance; and that punctuating question mark has proven to be a deceptive tool before, as in Hamlet' (I.v.40–41):

> . . . O my prophetic soul!
My uncle?

Could it be that these lines yearn to achieve, for strictly characterological reasons, quite a different sound, as follows:

> . . . O my prophetic soul!
> My uncle!

In *Othello* (at I.i.118) even an unmarked caesura can authorise the
value of silence in advancing the 'speaking' of the line. When
Brabantio calls Iago a 'villain' in the first act of the play, the super-
subtle Venetian quickly reacts by giving Desdemona's father his
appropriate honorific. Their heated conversation is poised to go
something like this, as Iago permutes Brabantio's angry and patri-
cian 'thou' to the icy civility of a class-conscious 'you'. Consider for
a moment what happens to the line when we assert the very
particular interpolation below:

Brabantio Thou art a villain.

Iago   You are [*pause*] a senator.

Beckett's dramaturgy will be highly informed by interventions like
these. For as his repertory develops and matures, so do his framing
devices for the playing of silence. In the theatre, as in music, there
will be no silence unless it finds a place for itself in the parenthesis
that exists between the sound of other sounds. Lines recited on
stage are in this respect both violators and conveners of silence; in
their delay and in their hesitation, in their absence as much as in
their presence, they mark silence, ironically, as acutely 'real'. On stage,
as Beckett has shown, following the path of master playwrights
such as Strindberg, Maeterlinck and especially Chekhov, silence
becomes a highly accomplished ventriloquist, capable of 'speaking'
for itself in many different tongues. It need no longer rely on a
steady stream of questionable adjectives only to say that it is really
something else. Words, Beckett's words, 'enough to exterminate a

regiment of dragoons', have been everywhere calculated on 'the Board' to make silence dramatically happen.[26]

Beckett's increasing sensitivity to their volubility can be traced not only in the printed directions for their delivery, an annotation that deepens and expands as the actor moves from *Godot* to *Endgame* to *Happy Days* to *Not I* and beyond, but even more so in the production notebooks the playwright, serving as his own director, kept for the stagings he supervised in London, Stuttgart, and Berlin.[27] This option simply does not exist in the case of Shakespeare (although it does exist to a certain extent in staging Brecht). Words in set repertory with silence and pause, as we have already seen in *Endgame* and *Happy Days*, will not be the only vehicles through which the sound of Beckett's 'Beckett' discovers its weight and volume, making itself heard. In the plays he wrote in the 1970s and 1980s, dialogue in the form of soliloquy and monologue will often be overwhelmed by the steady reliance on a far more comprehensive theatrical soundscape, revealing an unexpected urgency where time becomes negotiable in terms of stage space.

Here technology, most particularly in the form of the modulation accomplished through sophisticated electronic amplification, will be called upon to play its reciprocal part: chimes, heavy breathing, footfalls, the rocking of a chair, the knocking of a hand on a plain deal table, the closing of a book, or the notation a pencil makes on a notepad will establish and sustain the tonal quality appropriate for each new *mise-en-scène*. It will be lighting, however, rather than sound, surprisingly, that clarifies mood and atmosphere in this late style, even and especially when the space reveals, as in *Rockaby*, a seated figure whose few words – 'More' – play a stunning duet with an offstage voice previously recorded on tape, now broadcast as from some unspecified elsewhere.[28] In these short, complex plays, 'that MINE',[29] Beckett's image-making is at full stretch, tacitly admitting the enigma of light as it slowly fades to isolate, diminish, marginalise, fix and conceal. Such silence is well-spoken indeed.

iv

In the mechanical media Beckett's staging of silence will become even more mathematical and precise, sometimes calibrated to the micro-millisecond and 'every mute micromillisyllable'.[30] Here the coefficients can be splendidly timed but also anecdotal, as in the twenty-two-minute 'comic and unreal' *Film*, directed by Alan Schneider, where the close-up on a woman's 'sssh!', finger crossing lips, simultaneously repudiates and intensifies the palpable sound of this black-and-white movie's otherwise silent soundtrack.[31] With the playwright's move to television, the drama in the machine stylises technology one step further, offering the viewer uninterrupted access to the details of its own heady composition. In plays such as *Ghost Trio*, . . . *but the clouds* . . . and *Nacht und Träume*, Beckett finds a new vocabulary for silence, one primarily designed to suspend the moment for the digitally oriented. Structuring silence and letting it play in black and white and 'shades of the colour grey',[32] he fictionalises its enterprise and makes us wonder what happens to it as it crosses electronic borders. Recorded music fills in the gaps, surrounding and shaping words but also lending silence body, texture and, above all, volume. Silence never 'acted' quite like this before, Schubert and Beethoven notwithstanding. In . . . *but the clouds* . . . Beckett even makes us hear in silence as the transparency of a woman's face is deftly edited into the frame; when she lingers there in close-up soft focus, she mouths but does not speak the haunting closing lines of Yeats's 'The Tower', which we (and then the male voice-over) start to complete for her:

> *W's lips move, uttering inaudibly*: '. . . clouds . . . but the clouds . . . of the sky . . .', V *murmuring, synchronous with lips*: '. . . but the clouds . . .' *Lips cease. Five seconds.*[33]

Mallarmé would be suitably impressed; for it was, as he said, only in silence that music achieves its ideal fulfilment.[34]

No one who reads Beckett closely and sympathetically will fail to notice the details of his radiophonic sensibility. His is a full and complete grammar of listening. In his work for the BBC Radio Drama Department with Martin Esslin and Barbara Bray,[35] he ponders the aesthetics of the medium at the same time that he exploits it for practical advantage. In this electronic medium of pure sound, Beckett's vocabulary can become truly bizarre:

> Do you find anything . . . bizarre about my way of speaking? (*Pause.*) I do not mean the voice. (*Pause.*) No, I mean the words. (*Pause. More to herself.*) I use none but the simplest words, I hope, and yet I sometimes find my way of speaking very . . . bizarre. (*Pause.*)[36]

So sounds Maddy Rooney née Donne, the 'big pale blur', a formidable woman who must 'sound' fat just as her husband Dan must 'sound' blind. She quivers like a 'blanc-mange' and wonders whether her 'cretonne' is so unbecoming that she 'merge[s] into the masonry'. She is also the first of Beckett's destabilisers whose speech intrudes upon the organised presence of radiophonic white noise.

On these soundtracks silence will be both purposeful and percussive as it shapes into being the beat and tempo of an imagined world that insists on getting itself heard. 'I open . . . And I close,' intones a disembodied voice in the well-named *Cascando*; and 'I have come to listen,' says a shadowy character named She in *Rough for Radio I*.[37] Rather than hold it at bay, each voice distorts, vitalises, and animates silence, rendering it whole, giving it body and texture, making us hear the sound of *sound* as if for the first and only time – and for the last time, too, before it fades once more into the void. 'Joyce was a synthesiser,' Beckett shrewdly observed. 'I am an analyser.'[38]

V

Beckett's groundbreaking late fiction introduces us to the verbal equivalent of solitude. These lean and Spartan works establish a mysterious atmosphere everywhere empowered by new lines for 'recited' silence previously authorised in the dramas written for the mechanical media where, as he has shown, language knows full well how to pull the pin from the grenade. Especially in the first two volumes of a second trilogy comprising *Company*, *Ill Seen Ill Said* and *Worstward Ho*, 'silence' and 'stillness' demand to be read aloud, since much of their emotional resonance lodges in their tonality. In these lyrical works, as in the three-part *Stirrings Still*, the imperatives of silence, literally crying out loud, seek the sound of a human voice, a 'helping hand',[39] in order to formalise and elucidate the stubborn stillness of the universe. Now hear this:

> From where she lies she sees Venus rise. On. From where
> she lies when the skies are clear she sees Venus rise followed
> by the sun. Then she rails at the source of all life. On.
> At evening when the skies are clear she savours its star's
> revenge. At the other window. Rigid upright on her old
> chair she watches for the radiant one. Her old deal spindle-
> backed kitchen chair. It emerges from out the last rays and
> sinking ever brighter is engulfed in its turn. On. She sits on
> erect and rigid in the deepening gloom. Such helplessness
> to move she cannot help.[40]

vi

Wordsworth was lucky. When, in Book I of *The Prelude*, in a celebrated autobiographical passage, the young poet fixes his 'view / Upon the summit of a craggy ridge' and sees the mountain looming beyond, to the very 'horizon's utmost boundary', he opens his imagination and his canon to the power and the wonder, the mystery and the silence all around him.[41] Beckett's triumph over stillness (if indeed it is one) will be far 'less Wordsworthy'.[42] But it will be no less vexed, no less tentative, no less suspect, no less 'real', no less intuitive and no less seductive. A contemplative for sure, Beckett is, in this respect, like one of his own early tramps, something of a 'dud mystic', although he is far from being a fully credentialled romantic of 'the old style': no 'mystique raté', he just wants to find his text's final word.[43] 'Got it at last, my legend.' And *what is the word*?[44] Let us try to listen to it again:

. . . .
. . . .
. . . .
. . . .
. . . .
. . . .
. . . .
. . . .
. . . .
. . . .
. . . .
. . . .

After Beckett's 'Beckett' and his so *many* words for silence, 'so many words for silence' will never sound

. . . .

quite the same again.

CHAPTER 9

'Traces Blurs Signs': Where Beckett Meets Ibsen

i

'Can you stage a mouth?' Beckett wondered when he was thinking about a possible *mise-en-scène* for his play *Not I*, the first in a remarkable series of short works he wrote in the 1970s and the early 1980s, 'Just a moving mouth, with the rest of the stage in darkness?' 'The rest,' he concluded elsewhere, 'is Ibsen.'[1] Such a radical departure from the scenography we associate with one of the great inventors of modern European drama, who died the same year the Irish playwright was born, sets in motion Beckett's own late style for the theatre, one that continues to inform any director's use of stage space to this very day. And yet there may be much more to Beckett's revolutionary departure from the familiar conventions of stage realism than initially meets the eye. In his seemingly eccentric and exclusive dramaturgy, Beckett reveals his connection to Ibsen in odd and often surprising ways. Such 'traces blurs signs'[2] generally involve aspects of drama more formal than narrative: the use of offstage space, the evocative presence of music and other sounds as elements integral to the dramatic display (rather than mere framing devices), the coordination of props to highlight and advance the rising action, as well as the ephemeral inscription of ghostly presences to shape and problematise the character's – or in Beckett's case, the figure's – tantalising back-story. This chapter explores the several ways Ibsen's foundational theatre informs our understanding of Beckett's accomplishment at the same time that it suggests new ways to re-read Ibsen *after* and *because* of Beckett.

Let us begin with *John Gabriel Borkman*, Ibsen's penultimate play that he began writing in April 1896.[3] The first act opens on a *'living room, furnished in old-fashioned faded elegance'*, one of those hard-to-confuse interior spaces where 'great reckonings' are sure to take place.[4] Expansive and richly decorated, the decor immediately suggests additional venues where other dramas might be enacted:

In the background is an open sliding door, leading into the garden room with windows and a glass door. Through these, a view into the garden, where a snowstorm swirls in the dusk.[5]

How deftly Ibsen insinuates the tone and mood and atmosphere of some 'other space', outdoors, the cold mountain terrain of the final scene where Borkman meets his death as, symbolically, an 'ice hand' clutches at his heart. The observation of such technical mastery is one of the great rewards of reading Ibsen closely – and, as this example illustrates, in his case you can never read such mature texts too closely. Yet long before this drama reaches its cathartic *terminus ad quem* Ibsen has prepared his stage well to account for any number of significant and signifying elements crucial to the impact of *John Gabriel Borkman* in performance.

That opening scene begins in silence, although the silence has been calculated to speak volumes as we study the set where we encounter a seated female figure of a certain age. Alone on stage in her faded but once fashionable black dress, Mrs Gunhild Borkman is awaiting the arrival of her son Erhart. From the outside *'comes the sound of bells on a passing sleigh'* as Mrs Borkman listens, *'her eyes lighting up with joy'*. 'Erhart! At last!' she involuntarily whispers. It's a false start, however, for a surprise confrontation takes place when her long-estranged twin sister, the equally determined but now ailing catalyst figure, Ella Rentheim, appears in Erhart's place. What the text calls 'two shadows' suddenly takes centre stage as a dialogue loaded with subtext reveals a lifetime of deceit and barely repressed desire. Their Wagnerian duet (especially as played by Wendy Hiller and Peggy Ashcroft in the 1975 London production starring Ralph Richardson in the title role) proves to be yet one more diversion; for the drama in the text is sited elsewhere, in the sound of foot-steps, above. Ibsen's rhythmic footfalls upset all patterns previously established, becoming a new locus of dramatic intrigue. Ella Rent-heim has grossly miscalculated the stage effect of her melodramatic entrance:

Ella . . . perhaps I can see [Erhart]? And speak to him right now?

Mrs Borkman He hasn't come yet. But I expect him any minute.

Ella But, Gunhild – I'm sure he's here. I hear him walking upstairs.

Mrs Borkman (*with a quick upward glance*) Up in the salon?

Ella Yes. I've heard him walking up there ever since I came.

Mrs Borkman (*averting her eyes*) That's not Erhart, Ella.

Ella (*puzzled*) Not Erhart? (*Surmising.*) Who is it then?

Mrs Borkman It's him.

Ella (*quietly, with stifled grief*) Borkman! John Gabriel Borkman!

Mrs Borkman That's how he walks, up and down. Back and forth. From morning to night. Day in and day out.

Expanding the range and referentiality of the offstage space he has used with superb clarity and calculation before, Ibsen now makes use of a manufactured soundscape whose effects are meant to be both visceral and mysterious. Music, too, plays its part: the last measures of the 'Danse Macabre' play haltingly on a piano as 'footfalls', once again, ' . . . echo in the memory / Down the passage that we did not take . . .'[6]

It's all at once as though the material solidity of Ibsen's previous explorations of scenic and structural naturalism can no longer contain the passion let loose on this set, foreshadowing the complete breakdown of fourth-wall realism when, in the finale, the house and even the open land are '*lost to view*' as the landscape, with its slopes and ridges, '*alters slowly and becomes wilder and wilder*'. How we get from *there* to *here* in a mere four acts tells us a great deal about the dynamics of Ibsen's drama and its multivalent possibilities, defying any conventional notion of just what constitutes stage realism or the subversive interpretations that seek to deconstruct its upholstered theatricality.

John Gabriel Borkman further disturbs any easy definitions when it sets its various time signatures askew. Something odd happens between the acts when simultaneity and the play's vexed temporality are unexpectedly rendered in two competing dimensions. Stage time is compromised; we slowly recognise that each act beats to a slightly different clock. Only in the second act, which takes place in the well-lit upstairs salon furnished '*in austere Empire style*', are we introduced to the play's central character; obsessively pacing to and fro, he reveals himself as the source of those very same footfalls we have previously heard midway through the opening scene. And we now see that it is the young Frida, after all is said and done, who has been hard at work at her Saint-Saëns.

Such delayed exposition serves to solve one problem only to up the ante on another as, Stoppard-like, Ibsen systematises confusion and renders all safety and security lame. His technical proficiency may become transparent here, but its arresting effect in the first act remains just that: haunting and in this instance downright chilling, revealing Ibsen at his most gothic. Strindberg would take note – but perhaps that is going too far. *John Gabriel Borkman*'s reliance on the last measure of the 'Danse Macabre' meant that the Swedish playwright had to move in another musical direction for his own *Dance of Death*, a complex play of many textures that finally settles on Halvorsen's 'Entry of the Boyars' as an alternative.[7]

Beckett's footfalls in his 1976 play of the same name are rendered somewhat differently, as though we've suddenly arrived in the same performance space, only several years later. So much seems to have been taken away; the doctrine of 'less is more' has made a grim investment in assuring us that Beckett's 'less' is now firmly planted in exactly the right place. How tortured is the configuration on this skeletal, narrow space; a woman now paces back and forth, left to right, right to left, in what the text calls a *'clearly audible rhythmic tread'*, although May's motion alone, like Borkman's, is clearly 'not enough'.[8] At first glance Beckett's *Footfalls* appears to be an exquisite corpse of a drama, and a thorough undermining of everything Ibsen achieved in a work like *John Gabriel Borkman*. But not so fast – Beckett's eyes and ears may be just as attuned to the evocative potential of his medium, as the careful coordination of specifically theatrical sound effects soon makes clear. The lighting in this case is dim, *'strongest at floor level, less on body, least on head'*. A faint single chime emanating from some unspecified offstage elsewhere, followed by a potent pause as echoes slowly die, initiates the figure's ghostly movement, soon detailed by a female voice broadcast from the same tantalising elsewhere:

Watch how feat she wheels . . .
Seven, eight, nine, wheel.

Framed within the contours of a palpable stage darkness that may never have seemed quite so full before, May, like Ibsen's twin sisters, is an avid listener, too. And, strange as it may seem, on this stark platform she hears a great deal more than even they do. The second movement of the play finds her standing stock still in a highly mannered act of listening, fully facing front, stage right. In this

sombre tableau a disembodied voice is given all the words, a monologue which simultaneously describes and circumscribes a possible
back-story for what we have just seen represented on Beckett's
lonely stage:

> I say the floor here, now bare, this strip of floor, once was
> carpeted, a deep pile. Till one night, while still little more
> than a child, she called her mother and said, Mother, this
> is not enough. The mother: Not enough? May – the child's
> given name – May: Not enough. The mother: What do
> you mean, May, not enough, what can you possibly mean,
> May, not enough? May: I mean, Mother, that I must hear
> the feet, however faint they fall. The mother: The motion
> alone is not enough? May: No, Mother, the motion alone
> is not enough, I must hear the feet, however faint they fall.

Establishing Ibsen's and Beckett's credentials along the modernist/
late modernist/postmodernist divide here can be a tricky business.
Yet what I want to suggest is that this might be best accomplished
by looking closely at the specifics of their theatre language before
we begin to imagine what such specifics might be made or meant
to imply.

For Beckett as much as for Ibsen, it is the formal elements of
drama that articulate patterns of movement and meaning, allowing
always for the more practical and concrete articulation that must
take place in the instance of performance. Even a realistic play as
stylistically sure of itself as *A Doll's House* can demonstrate how
insistent the dramatic genre can be in maintaining a dialogue with
itself. Ibsen, the case in point, is never going to place a rocking
chair on his set, for example, unless someone is going to sit on
it, eventually, to emotionalise the setting. And Mrs Linde will
do exactly that as she fully commands the stage on her own, ripe
with anticipation and foreboding. She rocks back and forth –

irregularly, of course, and perhaps knitting, to boot – while we hear the sound of Nora dancing the tarantella at a holiday party offstage (unbeknownst to Nora, that Neapolitan spider-dance has her caught in a 'net' as lethal as the one that ensnares Lucky in his own very different dance in *Waiting for Godot*). Ibsen's denouement – Nora's *anagnorisis* as well as Torvald's and a marriage's undoing – is only a few moments away. How useful that simple rocking chair has been, therefore, in building the suspense that prepares us for the nineteenth century's most famous stage climax. Significantly, too, this drama will conclude with a bone-chilling offstage sound when Nora finally slams the door on the life she will leave behind.

Beckett, minimalist aesthete that he is, will be able to develop and sustain an entire dramatic universe based on the singular movement of a rocking chair. His 1981 play *Rockaby* (*Berceuse* in French), insists on an extreme economy in the performance situation, rendering Mrs Linde's position on stage, as well as the discursive *scène à faire* that follows it, all but baroque by comparison. Zeroing in on the essentials – in the case of *Rockaby* a chair, a seated female figure dressed in black and, above all, *'a faint shade of light'* – Beckett demythologises Ibsen and liberates him from the extraneous paraphernalia of the known world. 'All true grace,' as the playwright told Peter Hall in 1976 when he directed *Happy Days* at the National Theatre in London, 'is economical.'[9] And that is worth remembering. In *Rockaby*, as elsewhere, Beckett clears the deck, so to speak, yet in doing so he makes us appreciate all the more the value of a naturalistic set by focusing so deliberately on its remnants. What remains, as minimal as it can be, has to work overtime to compensate for all that has been left behind and, more to the point, blocked-out. Less is, once again, more; but in *Rockaby* that less is called upon to do what the drama itself calls a whole lot 'More'. Recited a full four times, that word is, in fact, the play's only 'live' dialogue. Full of technological complexity, the woman's recorded voice will be called on to play in agonising tandem with the synchronised movement of the chair, '*Rock and voice together*':

> till in the end
> the day came
> in the end came
> close of a long day
> when she said
> to herself
> whom else
> time she stopped
> *time she stopped*

What may look abstract in this particular display proves to be anything but so in performance (especially with a veteran Beckett actor such as Billie Whitelaw in the role). Yet what needs to be emphasised here is that, within the specialised vocabulary of theatre, this stage movement, both literal and figurative, is neither more nor less stylised than anything else that may have already been made to happen in an Ibsen play. What Beckett offers us within his careful calibration of stage machinery is, then, more of the same, only different; the dialogue theatre conducts with itself continues, decontextualised and recontextualised.

ii

Unlike James Joyce, who remained committed to Ibsen throughout his writing career, Beckett's attitude towards the Norwegian playwright was at best ambiguous (and even that's something of a stretch). He certainly never sat down to write him a fan letter that read in part: 'I am a young Irishman, eighteen years old, and the words of Ibsen I shall keep in my heart all my life.' Following the salutation 'Faithfully yours', the letter was signed 'Jas. A. Joyce'. Fascinated by Ibsen in 1900, the young Dubliner wrote a strong defence of *When We Dead Awaken* for the *Fortnightly Review*. Although the piece appeared in a small-circulation literary review, the article somehow found its way to the playwright, who appreciated Joyce's 'very benevolent' words and sent him a letter expressing his gratitude; the lines quoted above are part of an exchange between the two that would continue for three years.

Much later, when Joyce wrote about the theatre, which he did over a period of many years, he mentions Ibsen an impressive thirty-three times (Shakespeare's name being invoked seventeen times, George Bernard Shaw's a mere twelve).[10] In Beckett there is of course no similar hagiography. In his lengthy correspondence with Alan Schneider, for example, Ibsen is cited only in passing, as the director informs him about the work of the actors Jessica Tandy and David Warrilow on *Hedda Gabler* and *John Gabriel Borkman* in North America (Schneider further reports that during rehearsals for *Not I* for the world premiere at Lincoln Center in New York, he urged Tandy to think 'O'Neill rather than Ibsen over and over again').[11] Even during his Trinity years, Beckett's theatregoing at the Abbey included only an occasional Ibsen (we know, for example, that he saw *The Wild Duck* there in the early 1930s).[12] And in the unperformed *Eleutheria*, a '*drame bourgeois*' completed before *Waiting for Godot*, the best that can be said about Ibsen is that Beckett places him, parodically, in good company, along with Strindberg, Sophocles, Molière, W.B. Yeats, Hauptmann and Shakespeare.[13]

Any correspondence between these two theatrical giants must be found, then, if at all, in the 'traces blurs signs' enlivening their works in performance – and no more so than in the activation of other-worldly presences that quite overwhelm the visual and psychological horizons of their dramas. The Rat Woman in *Little Eyolf* and that very strange lady who enters from the sea, part mermaid, part woman – all this made spectacularly clear in Pam Gems's 2003 version performed by Natasha Richardson at the Almeida in London, under Trevor Nunn's expert direction – appear on Ibsen's platform to remind us that, despite the realistic tableau, there is always an 'other' world, sited in some offstage 'elsewhere'. The troll-like Hilde Wangel seems to come from such a place, and in the same play the master builder's wife, Aline Solness, seems to have been trapped there, too, and for many years, in what Beckett will later call in *Footfalls* 'her poor mind'. A transitional work like *The Wild Duck* even seems to suggest the spatialisation of such an 'elsewhere', the menagerie that lies just beyond reach, offstage. In all these instances, as in many others, Ibsen tries to make a bold and unnerving equation between his stage space and the space of human consciousness, although his approach remains tentative, anchored as it is in the unforgiving constraints of slice-of-life realism. But then slice-of-life realism always depends on just who's doing the slicing.

iii

In *Ghosts*, a play well named for the purposes of this discussion, the past is in the present, and in the future, too, as much as it will be a century later for O'Neill's tortured souls in *Long Day's Journey into Night*. For such characters 'the sun' always rises far too late, as it does for the terminally afflicted Osvald at the heart-wrenching conclusion of Ibsen's powerful family drama. Captain Alving, the late Court Chamberlain, haunts each character in this play, and his presence hovers over every action, looming every bit as large as the General's mighty portrait hanging in Hedda Gabler's drawing room. Here it is the ghost within that matters; wife, children and even that sanctimonious hypocrite Pastor Manders form a special victims' unit, fated as they are to retrace steps already taken. You know at once – or you should – that when a character early on in an Ibsen scene boldly asserts his paternity, as Engstrand does, by stating that he has the papers to prove it, long before the end of the drama it will be made crystal clear that he is nobody's biological father. Captain Alving, therefore, does not need to appear on stage at all, for he is already 'there' as he sets the scene on which the first act ominously falls. Regina and Osvald, his ill-informed offspring, merely play out their pre-assigned roles in an incestuous *pas de deux* as Mrs Alving watches on in growing recognition and horror.

> (*From the dining room comes the sound of a chair knocked over, along with Regina's voice in a sharp whisper.*)
>
> **Regina** Osvald! Are you crazy? Let me go!
>
> **Mrs Alving** (*starting in terror*) Ah – !
>
> (*She stares distractedly at the half-open door. Osvald is heard to cough within and start humming. A bottle is uncorked.*)
>
> **Manders** (*shaken*) But what happened, Mrs Alving? What was that?
>
> **Mrs Alving** (*hoarsely*) Ghosts.

Ibsen cleverly blocks the half-siblings' dance of death in another space, the dining room offstage, the better to focus our attention on where the real drama is to be found, in Mrs Alving's tortured mind. 'Ghosts', the one word she murmurs, even though it is stuck in her throat, says what Beckett will later call, simply and decisively: 'it all'.

Ibsen's great task in a drama like this is to establish his characters' history and complex motivation without resorting to the time-worn means of doing so. Soliloquy is out of the question in such a post-Scribean moment, as is the reliance on the physicalisation of ghostly presences who tread the boards (think *Hamlet* or *Macbeth* or *King Richard III* – Ibsen was surely thinking of them, for his work shows how well he knew this repertory). By the time of *Ghosts* those same revenants have now become internalised, although they serve, and efficiently so, similar dramatic purposes: advancing the plot, heightening the psychological texture, and serving as harbingers for what looks very much like fate. Ibsen's drama is therefore empowered when his characters are taken off guard by their ability to listen to long-repressed inner voices, and thus to communicate with the unseen.

It is in this sense that Beckett, particularly in his late works, picks up where a nineteenth-century writer such as Ibsen leaves off. Even as early as *Endgame* a character is struck almost dumb by 'something dripping' in his head, 'ever since the fontanelles'; that something turns out to be, not surprisingly, 'a voice'.[14] Krapp has his preserved electronically on magnetic tape; yet his recorded past, too, proves to be neither recuperated nor recaptured, merely one more device to cauterise the present in a deadly frame of voices when the ghosts in the machine cunningly (and fatally) reassert themselves. In late Beckett those same ghosts will be called upon to walk the stage once more, this time filtered through a few remaining gestures based on scenic and structural realism, as his characters desperately cry out for nothing less than 'More'.

iv

Beckett's ghosts appear in many guises. May, more 'semblance' than character in the classic Ibsen mould, is shrouded quite literally in a 'tangle of tatters' ('Grey rather than white, a pale shade of grey'), as she retraces her footsteps horizontally on a perilous journey across the stage. At 'nightfall', the voice-over intones, she passes before a prop we cannot see, a candelabrum, although the graphic image used to describe the invisible 'flames' is straight out of a gothic horror story: 'their light . . . like moon through passing rack'. In *Rockaby* 'subdued light', 'rest of stage dark', illuminates a 'prematurely old' female figure trapped and transfixed by the 'slight' and 'slow' movement of a chair that is 'controlled mechanically', without her 'assistance'. The space is defined by how the character inhabits it:

Black lacy high-necked evening gown. Long sleeves. Jet sequins to glitter when rocking. Incongruous flimsy head-dress set askew with extravagant trimming to catch light when rocking.

Is this what happens to seated figures like Mrs Linde and Gunhild Borkman when they wait too long on stage? In *Not I*, *That Time*, *A Piece of Monologue* and *Ohio Impromptu* such apparitions become even more stylised and remote. In the play whose epicentre was designed to be localised far, far away from all that 'rest' said to be, dismissively, so much Ibsen, a mouth – and Beckett does mean 'just a mouth' – is suspended on a proscenium '*eight feet above stage level, faintly lit from close-up and below, rest of face in shadow*'. As if this alarming image were not enough, *Not I* strategically stations a complementary 'figure', the larger-than-life Auditor, at stage right. Ghost-like shrouds are once again called upon to veil all that lies hidden beneath the surface:

Auditor, downstage audience left, tall standing figure, sex undeterminable, enveloped from head to foot in loose black djellaba, with hood, fully faintly lit, standing on invisible podium about four feet high shown by attitude alone to be facing diagonally across stage intent on Mouth, dead still throughout but for four brief movements where indicated.

In the next work, *That Time*, we are allowed to see even less, where less did not seem possible: darkness fades up to reveal only Listener's disembodied face '*about ten feet above stage level midstage off centre*'. It is an old '*white face*', as disruptive and provocative as anything we have previously seen on stage, with '*long flaring white hair as if seen from above outspread*' – as though we were now forced to look against our will at some ancient Ophelia gone to her watery grave. Yet this Listener is reactive and very much alive when voices A, B and C, '*his own*', assault him from both sides and above. In that very strange *A Piece of Monologue* where 'words are few', what the script specifies as '*faint diffuse light*' uncovers a spectral, white-haired Speaker who stands '*well off centre downstage audience left*' clad in '*white nightgown, white socks*'. A '*pallet bed*' is just visible stage right; and ten seconds before the end of speech the single lamplight begins – what else? – to fail. *Ohio Impromptu* delineates a landscape equally mysterious, constricted and confined, one of those strange Joycean 'rhymes' from *Ulysses* featuring 'two men dressed the same, looking the same, two by two'.[15] In the play we encounter the figures of Reader and Listener seated at a plain deal table while the rest of the stage is shrouded in a darkness that never felt quite so totalising. The rest of this 'earth', as Krapp says near his end, 'might be uninhabited'. Costumed in identical black coats and wearing wigs that feature the same long white hair, the figures in *Ohio Impromptu*, isolated but co-dependent, are, as the playwright indicates, '*as alike in appearance as possible*'. Ghosts indeed.

What is it, exactly, that Beckett seeks to represent by constructing such disturbing images on stage? While Ibsen may have been reluctant to transform his stage space so entirely into the space of human consciousness, preferring instead to *suggest* inner realities by presenting everything that points to them through the contrivance of staring in horror through an imaginary fourth wall – if something like this were to occur in the rhythm of everyday life, this is the way it might unfold (the best definition of realism on offer) – Beckett is far less ambivalent about making his characters physically confront their demons. Such a daring display on Beckett's part relies on an extremely selective use of elements earlier employed with a different sense of discretion and dramatic purpose in mind. Nowhere is this more in evidence than in the use of music and other sounds, and nowhere is this more efficiently accomplished than in Beckett's work in the mechanical media.

In *Ghost Trio* and *Nacht und Träume* Beckett, like Ibsen before him, incorporates specific musical motifs from the classical repertory and allows them to play an integral part in the making of his black-and-white television drama. In the first play the Largo of Beethoven's Fifth Piano Trio, the one in fact known as *The Ghost*, establishes the overall mood of frustrated expectation, and further serves to pinpoint the male character's reaction shots captured by the camera's alarming intensity. The one he waits for will not come; the tryst will not take place. Beckett is precise about the selection of particular measures, and exactly where and when they are to intrude, organising their elements in order to maximise their most percussive effects. The scoring of the text is therefore musically inspired, and such annotation serves to direct the figure's trio of actions: waiting, watching and listening. Ronald Pickup's choreographed movements made this especially poignant in the 1976 version broadcast on BBC in 'Shades'. In *Ghost Trio* silence, as always, is allowed to punctuate the affective nature of the screen's emerging soundcape; the on/off button on a cheap cassette is manipulated, sometimes abruptly, even clumsily by the seated figure who is recorded, just as Beethoven is, through the wonders of late-twentieth-century technology. *Ghost Trio* persuasively lets the silences linger, and these are among the play's most resonant moments.

Nacht und Träume returns the playwright's musical vocabulary to Schubert, whose 'Death and the Maiden' potently ironises the heavy tread of Maddy Rooney's footsteps as she trudges along the backroads on her journey to meet her husband Dan at the train station in the radio play *All That Fall*. In the much later drama for television, a male voice softly hums the last seven bars of Schubert's Lied, 'Nacht und Träume' (Op. 43, No. 2), which the composer based on a poem by the German romantic poet Matthäus von Collin:

. . . come again, holy night!
Sweet dreams, come again![16]

The only other 'voice' Beckett needs in *Nacht und Träume* belongs to silence, where the 'rest' is – and where night and dreams take place.

What should be immediately apparent from this discussion is the important role Beckett assigns to his musical motifs, as though they have finally been given the go-ahead to upstage even the characterological basis of the human drama itself. In *John Gabriel Borkman* the 'Danse Macabre' frames, even heightens and advances the action; in *Ghost Trio* and *Nacht und Träume* a Lied and a Largo go one step further: they become the most important players. Beckett works this transformation because he needs a stand-in for the very different dramatic world, the world of Ibsen, he and the art of his century have left far behind. And yet the 'traces blurs signs' remain, more vigorous and more spontaneous than anything we might have initially supposed. Beckett finds his unique dramatic voice by stretching Ibsen to the limits. The limits win. The rest is Beckett.

CHAPTER 10

Suitcases, Sand and Dry Goods

> *'Why doesn't he put down his bags?'*
> Estragon, *Waiting for Godot*

i

When Willy Loman, two large sample cases in hand, enters the set for *Death of a Salesman* in what is certainly one of the most famous walk-ons in modern stage history, he carries with him a whole lot of baggage.[1] That remarkable set was originally designed for the play's premiere on 10 February 1949 by the great Jo Mielziner, whose multi-platform concept provided an efficient solution to the tactical problem of communicating the *'air of . . . dream* [that] *clings to the place'* – *'a dream'*, as the playwright wrote, *'rising out of reality'*. Arthur Miller rarely tired of reciting the opening lines of the stage directions that set his drama in motion:

A melody is heard, played upon a flute. It is small and fine, telling of grass and trees and the horizon. The curtain rises.

As well he might, for the decisiveness of his scenography is a model of skilful stagecraft and deft stage management. Willy Loman's father made flutes, then sold on his own terms what he previously shaped, lovingly, with his own hands. Willy's sample case, heavy though it may be, contains only mass-produced dry goods hawked in Boston, Waterbury and other commercial markets up and down the vast New England territory traversed by the New York, New Haven and Hartford railway. The suitcase tells the whole story.

'A chair is just a chair,' Miller once observed about another foundational stage property, 'but place it on a stage and it becomes something else again.'[2]

I want to highlight that Loman suitcase, not only in terms of what Willy chooses to bring in it – and what he chooses to leave behind – but also in terms of what it offers an audience in terms of representation and recognition. It's a weighty item indeed, and not only because of the sample dry goods. Hidden somewhere in the side-pockets are the expensive silk stockings Willy presents to his mistress in a Boston hotel, a scene that will break his son's heart – and his own, signalling the beginning of the end for this tragedy of 'the common man', a man the playwright said was 'trying all the time to write his name on ice on a hot July day'.[3]

Part stage prop, part stage property, a familiar item such as a suitcase, part too of our everyday world, becomes 'something else again' once you ask your audience to study its provenance in a performance space,[4] where its resonances can be legion: arrival and departure surely, but also impermanence, fear of dispossession, a wandering to find home, dislocation and the absence of a fixed centre in a rapidly changing world, modernism gone haywire. Literary types like myself might be tempted to think of 'all this this here'[5] as symbolism, plain and maybe this time not so simple, although the dynamics of theatre reality, which demand the blunt literalism of material presence, would probably find such terminology lame. Literary symbolism dressed up like this, moreover, will be of absolutely no use to the actor, whose choices must be everywhere concrete and precise – and you can't *play* a symbol, as poor Nina discovers to her growing dismay when she tries to do so in the first act of *The Seagull*. John Gielgud commented on this unenviable situation when as a young actor he toured in the same play. Assigned the role of Chekhov's frustrated playwright-manqué Konstantin, who must place at the feet of his beloved the much-referenced seagull ('I am a seagull – no, no – I am an actress'), he complained, and rightly so: 'All I know about this business is that night after night I have to walk on stage with a dead bird in my hand. Simply horrible.'[6] Or, as Beckett might say, and in fact did say, 'no symbols where none intended'.[7]

Let us pause for a moment and think of Macbeth's speech about a famous murder weapon:

Is this a dagger which I see before me,
The handle toward my hand? Come, let me clutch thee:
I have thee not, and yet I see thee still.
Art thou not, fatal vision, sensible
To feeling as to sight? Or art thou but
A dagger of the mind, a false creation
Proceeding from the heat-oppressed brain?
I see thee yet, in form as palpable
As this which now I draw.[8]

In terms of the demands of the stage, as well as the aesthetics of the medium, which dagger is more real – *or how differently are they real* – the one that haunts Macbeth in his 'mind's eye' or the knife he holds in his hand by the end of this well-known speech? Each has a tantalising momentum of its own, dramatically speaking, and Shakespeare can be counted on to take maximum advantage of both. But the concrete form, as Gielgud noted, the same one the assistant stage manager has to worry about night after night after night, is always going to be the real teaser. The profoundly figurative verbal image, designed as it is to capture the imagination, has an intoxicating innocence about it, untouched, untouchable and inviolate – ungraspable, finally, by audience and protagonist alike. Perhaps this dagger actually is in some fundamental psychological sense 'more real because imagined' (it certainly remains so for Macbeth).

But this is not the down and dirty business of theatre. While poetry is, *pace* Marianne Moore, about 'imaginary gardens with real toads in them', drama, especially in the sense that I am talking about it in this chapter, requires that both the gardens and the toads be real.[9] And they have to be staged; this is a constructed reality if there ever was one. That is what Alain Robbe-Grillet meant when he said, speaking of Beckett, that the *donnée* of theatre lies in the fact that it is palpably and emphatically *there*.[10] For 'daggers of the mind' of the sort that taunt Macbeth, on the other hand, there will be no *there* there.

We might therefore be encouraged to look elsewhere to describe that 'something' that takes its 'course' on stage;[11] and the audience might indeed just find that 'something' in the rich dialogue that drama matters like this one insist on having with themselves. A play such as *Death of a Salesman* or *Waiting for Godot*, while suggesting that it could also be about many other things, is in some fundamental sense principally about itself as a work for the theatre. Consider the suitcase; Chekhov most certainly did. In *The Cherry Orchard* Madame Ranevsky arrives late at night from Paris and immediately enquires about her luggage: 'Has someone gone to the station?'[12] At the end of the play the same cases, previously hidden discreetly offstage, are now in full view and very much frontal, bringing closure to the drama in a neat but unobtrusive framing device. And in that last scene another character, the always-busy Varya, is discovered alone on stage 'regarding' the suitcases, securing locks and inscribing labels; we regard the suitcases with her, looking at *her* looking, but then looking at the suitcases too, something like looking with eyes on both sides of our heads. But then you always know that rigid definitions of what you're supposed to be seeing through the imaginary fourth wall of a staged realism like this is in big trouble when characters start talking to the props. As indeed they do: 'Dear old bookcase,' Raneskaya intones early on, kissing the shelves along the way. 'My little desk . . . ' she rhapsodises, never completing the thought – but allowing us to do so. Thank God for the ellipsis. By the next morning and the next scene you're no longer surprised that Liubov Andreyevna is talking to the cherry trees. This is, after all, the play its author subtitled 'A Comedy in Four Acts'.

Chekhov is a case in point, and a good one at that. His characters are for ever on the move. In the four major plays he wrote in the last decade of his life (he was only forty-four when he died), catalyst figures arrive from exotic-sounding places like Paris, Moscow and even provincial Harkov to disturb the ordinary texture of everyday life on a country estate located – how shall I say? – elsewhere. And in the vastness of Russia in the time in which these plays take place that means very far away indeed. Things change when writers and actresses and 'lovesick' majors invade such pastoral settings, albeit rundown and gone to seed, just as they do when self-delusional professors arrive on the scene. 'Ah, there's a professor for you,' cries out *Dyaya* Vanya in the half-parodic, half-envious tirade he delivers in the drama's opening moments, 'a man who never tires of lecturing on subjects that intelligent people know already, and the dumb ones aren't interested in anyway . . . '. The familiarity and the predictability and the security of everyone's routine is ungenerously and all at once upended. The tea boils over in the samovar. Meals must be prepared, and elaborate ones at that, served at odd times, too. Someone sings a rowdy folk tune to the strumming of a balalaika; they're told to shut up, for the professor is unwell and 'the great man' needs his rest. 'It's a long time since I've tasted noodles,' the old nurse laments in the same play, 'sinner that I am.'

Departures are equally calibrated in this repertory for maximum dramatic effect; and in Chekhov's case they have been celebrated for taking up the entire last act. In one farewell scene a female figure (described with deadly accuracy as 'too indolent to move') uses up several minutes of stage time wondering just how to say goodbye. 'Well, for once in my life!' Yelena sighs in *Uncle Vanya* as she falls into Astrov's warm embrace. Then she takes his pen.

Nobody – and I mean nobody – goes quietly in Chekhov, for these turn-of-the-century Russians are nothing if not great talkers. Maxim Gorky got it right when he said that this playwright certainly understood 'the tragic import of life's trivialities'.[13] In the meantime, suitcases need to be packed.

So much to-ing and fro-ing within a Chekhov play involves the manipulation of a great deal of stage machinery, but within the modern realistic tradition of which his work serves as a primary example some items prove to be more durable than others. Even Peter Brook, who directed *The Cherry Orchard* in period costume but on a wide proscenium without walls, substituting his signature rugs in their place, could not entirely abandon Madame Ranevsky's bags in his minimalist scenography. In his 1988 production seen at the Brooklyn Academy they remained a forceful visual reminder of what Chekhov's characters fear most, but what something like fate forces them to face: dispossession and loss. 'All Russia is our garden,' one character muses, then memorialises, as he attempts to emblematise the old Russia quickly being despoiled. Hannibal is at the gates. When the trees fall to the axe, you pack what you can. Or, like old Firs, the retainer who still thinks of himself as a serf, you risk being forgotten and left behind.

Tom Stoppard ambitiously traces some of the same lost territory in *The Coast of Utopia*.[14] In this sprawling three-part invention, *Voyage*, *Shipwreck* and *Salvage*, nineteenth-century Russian thinkers, anarchists and political revolutionaries – expatriates all, exiles really – are similarly on the move as they seek safe haven, criss-crossing time and space in cities as far apart as Moscow, Paris, Nice, London, St Petersburg and Geneva, although they begin their wandering at Premukhino, the Bakunin family estate featuring one more faded/fated garden, this one located a hundred and fifty miles north-west of Moscow. Each part of the trilogy begins with an emblem of all that has been lost: the image of a sullen man holding a child's glove, high above a rolling sea; you can even imagine hearing the whooshing sounds of winds and ocean waves, and a distant clanking bell. Stoppard's refugees never reach their utopias, their longed-for nowheres – at best, bag and baggage in hand, they only get a glimpse of the shore. 'It's all right,' the progressive and pro-western Alexander Herzen concludes, movingly, at the end of the trilogy, 'we don't have to kill the myopic in our myopia.'

And yet it is Miller's contemporary Tennessee Williams who seems to have understood most profoundly the psychological peril of carrying too much baggage with you. 'They told me to take a streetcar named Desire, and then transfer to one called Cemeteries and ride six blocks and get off at – Elysian Fields!'[15] The irony cuts deep as Williams's most mythic – and most fragile – female figure makes her stage entrance:

> *Blanche comes around the corner, carrying a valise. She looks at a slip of paper, then at the building, then again at the slip and again at the building. Her expression is one of shocked disbelief. She is daintily dressed in a white suit with a fluffy bodice, necklace and earrings of pearl, white gloves and hat, looking as if she were arriving at a summer tea or cocktail party in the garden district . . . There is something about her uncertain manner, as well as her white clothes, that suggests a moth.*

Eunice's trenchant greeting could not be more piercing: 'What's the matter, honey? Are you lost?'

In *A Streetcar Named Desire* Blanche is, of course, only famously 'passing through'. Her downward trajectory leads from Belle Reve – 'beautiful dream' – to her fatal sojourn at Elysian Fields after the final indignity of being caught in the arms of one more inappropriate lover, this time in a one-night stand with an under-age high school boy – as though the killer of opening a door on her naked young husband in bed with another man were not enough to send her off packing on such a perilous journey. No wonder she recoils from the harsh light of everyday reality. As she tells Mitch, the most unlikely of beaus:

> I don't want realism. I want magic! . . . Yes, yes, magic!
> I try to give that to people. I misrepresent things to them.
> I don't tell truth, I tell what *ought* to be truth. And if that
> is sinful, then let me be damned for it! – *Don't turn the*
> *light on!*

All of this played out against the background music of 'Paper Moon', the popular tune that drives the drama forward without overtaking it: ' . . . *and it wouldn't be make-believe if you believed in me*'. '*Flores para los muertos*' (flowers for the dead) have an ugly way of insinuating their presence in any and every Garden-of-Eden world, no matter how brilliantly – I almost said how desperately – constructed.

Stella-for-star, the younger DuBois sister, has found another sort of refuge from the past, hers in the bed of the poker-playing hunk Stanley Kowalski: 'The game is a seven card stud.' Blanche's 'valise' – the word as carefully chosen as her moth-like persona and the unsullied whiteness of her name – contains the few remnants she can salvage from a questionable past – cheap knock-off goods, fake furs, costume jewellery, a rhinestone crown – and only her macho, meat-throwing brother-in-law, as much a grotesque as she has become, is temporarily fooled by their valorisation. While they last (that is, before Stanley gets his hands on them), Blanche uses the contents of her suitcase to perform one last *ballo in masquera* (this drama is, after all, set quite deliberately in Mardi Gras New Orleans). But this carnivalesque road show, played out, is about to end; Mr Shep Huntleigh does not keep his appointment. A Doctor and a Matron appear instead as Blanche DuBois – deluded? triumphant? a little bit of both? – is led offstage in her 'Della Robbia blue'. But not before she recovers her regal voice to deliver the American theatre's most memorable line: 'Whoever you are – I have always depended on the kindness of strangers.' Needless to say, her suitcase has been packed for the last time.

ii

Playwrights like Miller and Williams and Chekhov luxuriate in a wide theatre vocabulary to speak elegantly and persuasively on its own terms, and to do so accessibly within the public domain. Writing in a specialised genre that depends for its life on the physicality of bodies in motion and the vocalisation of speech – writing, in short for the spoken voice – Miller once said that he began his career by shouting all the lines out loud. Later, he said, he could do this inside his head.[16] But accomplished writers for the stage also know when to let the objects do the talking. Even the loquacious Lady Bracknell in *The Importance of Being Earnest*, whose hyper-articulateness is said to mirror Oscar Wilde's own – knows when to step aside when another sort of suitcase, in this case a handbag found on the Brighton Line ('the line, Mr Worthing, is immaterial') is sufficient unto itself for wrapping up the play in a hilarious eleventh-hour denouement.

Other writers have been far more circumspect in their exploration of this particular virtue of the stage. And none more so than Samuel Beckett. 'Joyce was a synthesiser,' he once observed in a rare instance of self-revelation already cited in this text. 'I am an analyser.'[17] Beckett may always seem to be writing a hundred thousand years after everybody else, but a careful review of his work reveals that it is energised by the same considerations and a clever updating of some of the same stage conventions. In *Waiting for Godot*, the one Beckett drama everybody knows – or at least knows about – it is the much put-upon Lucky who plays the carrier and minder of stool, basket and bags. In reality, his master claims, 'he carries like a pig. It's not his job.'[18] Perhaps this character is called

Lucky because he is lucky to have 'no expectations'[19] – either about himself or about anything or anyone else. Still, Beckett's tramps are worried about him. 'Be careful,' Pozzo warns them, although they take no heed. 'He's wicked – with strangers.' Gogo can't figure out why Lucky doesn't 'put down his bags' after Pozzo – his name a dead ringer for ambiguity (the Italian phrase '*è un pozzo di sapienza*' means 'he's a fountain of learning', while a '*pozzo nero*' is a cesspool) – decides to 'dally' with them:

> You want to know why he doesn't put down his bags, as you call them. . . .You are sure you agree with that? . . . The answer is this. But stay still, I beg of you, you're making me nervous! . . . Good. Is everybody ready? Is everybody looking at me . . . [*To Lucky.*] Will you look at me, pig! Good . . . I am ready. Is everybody listening? Is everybody ready? . . . I don't like talking in a vacuum. Good. Let me see . . . What was it exactly you wanted to know? [*Gogo repeats the question.*] Don't interrupt me! If we all speak at once we'll never get anywhere . . . What was I saying? . . . What was I saying? . . . Ah! . . . Why he doesn't make himself comfortable? Let's try and get this clear. Has he not the right to? Certainly he has. It follows that he doesn't want to. There's reasoning for you. And why doesn't he want to? . . . Gentlemen, the reason is this [*Didi urges Gogo to make a note of this.*] . . . He wants to impress me, so that I'll keep him . . . Perhaps I haven't got it quite right. He wants to mollify me, so that I'll give up the idea of parting with him. No, that's not exactly it either . . . He wants to cod me, but he won't . . . He imagines that when I see how well he carries I'll be tempted to keep him on in that capacity . . . He imagines that when I see him indefatigable I'll regret my decision. Such is his miserable scheme. As though I were short of slaves! . . . Atlas, son of Jupiter!

Heisenberg's uncertainty principle, Niels Bohr notwithstanding, has rarely been rendered quite so flamboyantly (and to top it off, Pozzo gets the classical allusion wrong).[20] But what is it – exactly – that the unfortunate Lucky carries so pathetically in those suitcases, back and forth, stage right to stage left, then, in a sorely diminished state, stage left to stage right? They certainly take up a great deal of time – which of course would have passed anyway, as the characters are quick to assure us, but 'not so fast'; yet no one before Beckett would have thought of putting bags and baggage into so much play. Before we learn for sure what we have long suspected – that Godot isn't coming, not now and perhaps never – 'the key word in my play', the author once said, is 'perhaps'[21] – the contents of the bags turn out to be sand.

Miller and Beckett (each is certainly the other's *un-*), may at first sight seem like a highly unusual pairing. And yet their two great plays, *Death of a Salesman* and *Waiting for Godot*, though composed an ocean apart, one in Brooklyn and the other on the rue St Jacques on the Left Bank in Paris, were both completed by the same *annus mirabilis*, mid-century 1949. Each play gave its postwar audience in the western world a new visual language for understanding itself. Seeking compositional order in spaces where it does not necessarily present itself, Beckett's theatre, unlike Miller's, inhabits and stage-manages enormous empty spaces where stage light has as much weight as stage character. Often the point of Beckett's stage image, especially in his late style for the theatre, is simply hard to fathom, although like Miller and the other playwrights mentioned above, he is always in search of an image to describe the world we live in and the way we live in it now.

The worlds they represent on stage have been scarred for ever by the ghosts of many other suitcases, the lost luggage their owners were never able to retrieve. What was in all those empty suitcases piled mountain-high by Nazi murderers and their self-serving collaborators at Auschwitz and other European prison camps for mass extermination? Even more horrifying to contemplate, where are their contents now? 'We know a little something about the human race that we didn't know before,' Fania says in *Playing for Time*, Miller's adaptation of Fénelon's *The Musicians of Auschwitz*, 'And it's not good news.'[22]

Seen in this light, a play like *Waiting for Godot* can be a whole lot more disturbing than the absurdist or existential display it is sometimes claimed to be. Beckett's defoliated landscape, a rock and a single tree, was all too real for far too many refugees seeking asylum after the so-called European 'theatre' of a world war, or in the radioactive aftermath of the deadly bombing in Hiroshima. Weapons of mass destruction indeed. Those civilians who picked themselves up and marched away after so much devastation carried suitcases, too – and they were supposed to have been the lucky ones. Who knows? When we sit down to write the history of theatre in the second half of the twentieth century, Beckett, not Miller, may turn out to be the ultimate realist after all.

Beckett, moreover, as Harold Pinter shrewdly observed, 'leaves no maggot lonely'.[23] Even in *Endgame* – a play its author called 'as dark as ink',[24] the dark underside of *Godot* – when Clov's bags are packed and ready to go, the curtain falls before this stage character exercises his option to depart. In the earlier play, Godot doesn't *come*; in this one Clov doesn't *go*. Like Hamm – the Ham-let and the ham actor – Clov, like the rest of us, somehow hesitates to end. No one walks out on anyone else in this repertory, even when a suitcase is ready at hand. Instead, they stay the course. Stage direction: *They do not move.*[25]

'Hopeless thing sand,' Joyce has Leopold Bloom say in *Ulysses*. 'Nothing grows in it. All fades.' This Jewish wanderer in Ireland then traces 'I AM. A' with his finger in the same sand, a message he soon effaces.[26] Beckett has his Lucky, his 'knook' ('a word invented by me', he admitted[27]) carry such effacement in a suitcase, and those of us who are still thinking about Beckett are still trying to figure out what the message in the sand might be. Erasure like his looms large; and although we recognise that 'less is more',[28] as this playwright has demonstrated, it only can be so if that less is in the right place, packed up neatly in a suitcase as it is.

It is, then, Lucky's suitcase, like Willy Loman's, that matters most. The sheer persistence of carrying it on stage in so many different ways, and to such different dramatic effect, links such players even more so to their fellow travellers in the drama of their century: the brother whose box contains the props for three-card monte and the brother who carries and covets a money-filled stocking in Suzan-Lori Parks's *Top Dog/Under Dog*; the post-*Death of a Salesman* salesmen whose attaché cases unfold phoney contracts for worthless land in Mamet's *Glengarry Glen Ross*; the suburban mom with the matching set who returns to her deconstructed kitchen in Sam Shepard's *True West* after her trip to Alaska and finds toasters everywhere; the feckless denizens of Shaw's *Heartbreak House*, where luggage lies strewn about everywhere, still unpacked; the family matriarch in Lorraine Hansberry's *A Raisin in the Sun*, whose bags wait for her offstage while she re-enters the set at the very last moment to retrieve a plant still yearning for light; Claire Zachanassian in Dürrenmatt's *The Visit*, who returns to her place of origin with ample trunks in order to exact a brutalising revenge; Andreas in Brecht's *Galileo*, whose satchel hides the scientific truths he will smuggle out of Italy across the Alps; and Tony Kushner's Hannah Pitt, who brings her tote on a Greyhound bus all the way from Salt Lake to Greenwich Village on a mission to save her son, and herself, in *Angels in America* – all of this in 'sin city', the ever-fascinating Sodom and Gomorrah she discovers in New York, but where there is also an odd kind of redemption at the Bethesda Fountain in Central Park. Setting her suitcase aside, this lapsing Mormon nurtures her son's would-be lover's former lover; and no sooner does Prior Walter, the last of that name, recite a line we have all heard before, camping it up ('I have always depended on the kindness of strangers'), than this pragmatic

Utah Westerner is ready to counter it with, 'Why, that's a very foolish thing to do.'[29]

We will find much more of the same as stage characters are scripted to arrive in other unlikely places, as they do in O'Neill's *Anna Christie* and Albee's *Everything in the Garden*; when they are slated to embark on journeys that will only bring them back to where they came from, as in Horton Foote's *The Trip to Bountiful* or across the several decades spanning August Wilson's cycle of Pittsburgh plays; or when they have set out to explore territories yet unknown, as in Clifford Odets's legendary *Awake and Sing!* – or even more significantly, when Nora slams the door in *A Doll's House* and walks out on a marriage and a house built on nothing but sand. And then there are the curious figures who appear on stage, uninvited, unwanted and – in a rare thing for Italians – unembraced, carrying a different but no less potent sort of baggage – Pirandello's six characters metatheatrically searching for an author. 'Where do we go from here?' one Beckett-like player asks, as he will again in Tom Stoppard's *Rosencrantz and Guildenstern Are Dead*.[30] In the vast trajectory of unfolding events, and in the way in this instance drama has an uncanny way of referring us back to what we have already seen it do before, *the same but different*, the answer is an unequivocal Beckettian: 'ON.' And on and on and so on.

Despite Pozzo's fateful recommendations in his weighty speeches from *Godot*, playwrights who aim to make a difference in how we think continue to reference their world – our world – in their scrupulous playing with time. 'I could not imagine a theatre worth my time,' Miller wrote in his autobiography *Timebends*, 'that would not want to change the world.'[31] Beckett, even more so perhaps – and this according to cultural critics who run the gamut from Susan Sontag to Gilles Deleuze to Adorno, not to mention most writers who care about their craft – is rightly credited for creating for his audience nothing less than a new way of thinking. Drama matters; attention, attention must finally be paid, even to such small things as suitcases, sand and dry goods. Theatre language may very well be a world unto itself, but as a public medium that plays itself out in the public forum it traces the lineaments of our world, too, and makes us rethink who we are. It makes us see ourselves better, even and most especially so when it makes us recognise, lurking somewhere behind the curtains – that void – what we may least like to see revealed. *See better*, the Beckett text advises, *Fail better*.[32]

Virgil knew this long ago. When his mythic wanderer Aeneas, longing to find a home, a still centre in a world as changing as ours surely is, stops on his Mediterranean voyage and contemplates the artwork on a temple in Carthage representing the sorrow and the pity of yet another war, this one in Troy, he has him murmur '*sunt lacrimae rerum*' – 'these are the tears of things'.[33] Pozzo plays this somewhat differently:

> The tears of the world are a constant quantity. For each
> one who begins to weep somewhere else another stops. The
> same is true of the laugh . . . Let us not then speak ill of our
> generation, it is not any unhappier than its predecessors . . .
> Let us not speak well of it either . . . Let us not speak of it
> at all.

And then Beckett, like Virgil before him, lets his audience complete the thought: '*et mentem mortalia tangunt*' – 'and our mortality cuts to the heart'.

ADDENDUM

To What? The No-Thing That Knows No Name and the Empty Envelope Blissfully Reconsidered

> *'I love talking about nothing.*
> *It is the only thing I know anything about.'*
> Oscar Wilde, *An Ideal Husband*

i

In July 1974, when Maurice Beebe planned to edit a special number of the *Journal of Modern Literature* to interrogate (as we *didn't* say at the time) a sea change that was taking place in the cultural landscape all around us, he already knew that such a consideration was long overdue. 'From Modernism to Post-Modernism', as the 200-page issue of *JML* was called, served as an early and modest and now mostly forgotten contribution to an academic discussion that was to have major repercussions in the decades to come. Thirteen years later Linda Hutcheon published her seminal study, *A Poetics of Postmodernism: History, Theory, Fiction*, soon followed in 1991 by Frederic Jameson's provocative and influential response entitled *Postmodernism: The Cultural Logic of Late Capitalism*. At about the same time Marjorie Perloff and others began to wonder whether one could effectively talk about 'postmodern genres', while Deborah Geis speculated on the specifically theatrical potential of 'postmodern theatric[k]s' in contemporary American drama. A little later, critics such as H. Porter Abbott would centre this discussion – and appropriately so – on Beckett. Could his work be properly situated in the broad and less contentious context of 'late modernism'? Richard Begam went even further, describing how Beckett's fiction anticipates many of the defining themes and ideas of Barthes, Foucault and Derrida in moving us towards 'the end of modernity'.[1]

By contrast, Beebe's authors were far more tentative in the approaches they pursued, although it should be noted here that they were equally concerned, albeit in embryonic form, with the interrelated questions of aesthetics, Marxism, literary form and culture (though in this case it is probably fair to say that theirs was more observation than critique). Looking back on the period when these accomplished essays were written in the early 1970s seems like a glance at a lost innocence, soon to be characterised as nothing short of critical naivety – for the special issue appeared in print in the fleeting moment just before literary theory took over literature departments with a vengeance. Translators from the French were working overtime. Modernism, ill-defined, and postmodernism, even more so – the latter term continues its vexed reign, this despite the consolations derived from those ambitious studies cited above – was a tempting though still ambiguous borderline for the *JML* authors, centring their attention as they did on an uncontested canonical space of 'primary' texts: Eliot, Pound, William Carlos Williams, Wyndham Lewis, Lawrence and Gertrude Stein loom large. 'The remarks that follow,' Beebe wrote cautiously in his introduction, 'are therefore intended to be more suggestive than definitive.'[2]

My own contribution to the volume was a short piece that served, as this one does, as the final entry but not the final word on an intellectual dilemma that was at best both playful and profound. 'The Empty Can: Samuel Beckett and Andy Warhol', composed soon after completing my PhD during the time when I was still trying to figure out how *not* to think about this most formidable of Irish playwrights, ended, *pace* Cleanth Brooks,[3] like this:

> The well-wrought urn may have indeed become the empty can, but in the transformational historical process this anxiety between object and audience has become a terrifying

metaphor for the anxiety the world imposes on us as we approach the final quarter of twentieth-century aesthetics.[4]

Shades of Harold Rosenberg, self-quotation notwithstanding. In his 1964 study, *The Anxious Object: Art Today and Its Audience*, Rosenberg made a persuasive case for an unenviable condition Beckett had earlier problematised in his novel *Watt*: 'But what was this pursuit of meaning, in this indifference to meaning? And to what did it tend? These are delicate questions.'[5] A Beckett play – *Endgame*, for example – and a series of Warhol silkscreens, both filled with alarming and mysterious suggestion, might be seen as objects 'anxious' for a definition nowhere to be found. In terms of audience reception, nothing might indeed be more *sur*-real than nothing.

The 1970s was also an important decade for a change – nothing less than a paradigm shift – that was taking place in Beckett's creative activity. His late style for the theatre achieved a startling new dimension with Jessica Tandy's performance of *Not I* at Lincoln Center in New York in 1972. This was followed a few months later by Billie Whitelaw's legendary interpretation at the Royal Court in London (a well-known version shot in close-up sharp focus was broadcast on the BBC as part of the programme called 'Shades' in 1976). Beckett had written a remarkable play about a mouth in conflict with a stubborn pronoun, first-person, then – even more terrifying, ' . . . she . . . SHE! . . . '. Other body parts were soon on display. Beckett's next play, *That Time*, featured a disembodied head in a work the playwright himself characterised as related to *Not I*.[6] That play was produced in 1976 on a double bill, also at the Royal Court, with an even more enigmatic piece, *Footfalls*. In the second of the play's three related movements, an offstage voice intones fragments of a story that seem to objectify the haunting soundscape we encounter on stage as a female figure paces back and forth:

I say the floor here, now bare, this strip of floor, once was carpeted, a deep pile. Till one night, while still little more than a child, she called her mother and said, Mother, this is not enough. The mother: Not enough? May – the child's given name – May: Not enough. The mother: What do you mean, May, not enough? May: I mean, Mother, that I must hear the feet, however faint they fall. The mother: The motion alone is not enough? May: No, Mother, the motion alone is not enough, I must hear the feet, however faint they fall.[7]

In the next section the shrouded figure, '*chime a little fainter still*', narrates a 'semblance' of what may be her highly charged but nonetheless compromised back-story:

Mrs W: You yourself observed nothing . . . strange?
Amy: No, Mother, I myself did not, to put it mildly.
Mrs W: What do you mean Amy, to put it mildly, what can you possibly mean, Amy, to put it mildly? Amy: I mean, Mother, that to say I observed nothing . . . strange is indeed to put it mildly. For I observed nothing, of any kind, strange or otherwise. I saw nothing, heard nothing, of any kind. I was not there. Mrs W: Not there? Amy: Not there.[8]

Beckett's short prose published in the same period, written in an eccentric 'grammar for being elsewhere',[9] was in some ways even more elliptical – and nothing if not downright 'strange'. It was difficult to tell at the time whether these short pieces were discrete works of their own, works in progress, or fragments of some larger opus yet to emerge, re: Joyce.

ii

With so many parallels to Dada composition, echoes of James Joyce, and resonances to the 'midget grammar'[10] of Gertrude Stein, it has always been difficult to know where to place Beckett on the great modernist/postmodernist divide. Somewhere beyond minimalism, his work explores the vast terrain that separates nothing from nothingness, and both from the far more intriguing *nothing in particular*. How can 'worsening words', Beckett's literary métier, be structured, repositioned and retooled so that they 'enclose' – embrace really – something as contagious and all-encompassing as:

this this –
this this here –
all this this here –[11]

In the early 1970s 'The Empty Can' proposed looking elsewhere, outside literature perhaps, for the appropriate artistic climate of spontaneity that seemed central to Beckett's relentless 'work-in-regress'.[12]

Undaunted by such considerations, as well as several others, Beebe mailed a copy of the journal to Beckett. A few weeks later he called to say that an airmail letter addressed to me c/o the *Journal of Modern Literature*, Temple University, Philadelphia, had just arrived at his office, posted from Paris. But there was something odd about this: what he held in his hand was only an empty envelope, *nothing* enclosed. Perhaps, he offered, a letter had slipped out? Interesting: I asked if the envelope looked as though it had been sealed. Apparently not. Did I want it sent to me anyway? I told the journal editor to dispatch it sans delay.

The Beckett envelope arrived by fast-mail the very next day. I recognised both the hand and the handwriting immediately. The void never looked quite so promising before, especially so for a young scholar who was beginning to find his way through so much 'mental thuggee'. *A pox on void.*[13]

Such was my first contact with Samuel Beckett: nothingness enclosed indeed. Yet what the receipt of his non-correspondence makes clear, finally, is something much more substantial and fulfilling than the provenance of some empty can: fashions of critical definition come and go, yet the encounter with Beckett's magnificent void, 'that MINE', is still out there somewhere waiting for his Reader, as for his Listener – somehow, 'nohow',[14] something to think about, always already *not* there.

WORKS CITED

Abel, Lionel. *Metatheatre: A New View of Dramatic Form* (New York: Hill & Wang, 1963).

Ackerley, C.J. *Demented Particulars: The Annotated Murphy* (Tallahassee: Journal of Beckett Studies Books, 1998).

——— and S.E. Gontarski. *The Grove Companion to Samuel Beckett* (New York: Grove, 2004).

Albright, Daniel. *Beckett and Aesthetics* (Cambridge: Cambridge University Press, 2003).

———. *Representation and the Imagination: Beckett, Kafka, Nabokov, and Schoenberg* (Chicago: University of Chicago Press, 1981).

Amiran, Eyal. *Wandering and Home: Beckett's Metaphysical Narrative* (University Park: Pennsylvania State University Press, 1993).

Banville, John. *The Sea* (London: Picador, 2005).

———. *The Untouchable* (New York: Vintage, 1998).

Barale, Michèle Aina and Rubin Rabinovitz, eds. *A KWIC Concordance to Samuel Beckett's Trilogy: 'Molloy', 'Malone Dies' and 'The Unnamable'*, 2 vols. (New York: Garland, 1988).

Barthes, Roland. *A Lover's Discourse: Fragments*, trans. Richard Howard (New York: Hill & Wang, 1979).

Beauman, Sally. *The Royal Shakespeare Company: A History of Ten Decades* (Oxford: Oxford University Press, 1982).

Beckett, Samuel. *As the Story Was Told: Uncollected and Late Prose* (London: John Calder, 1990).

———. *Collected Poems 1930–1978* (London: John Calder, 1986).

———. *Collected Poems in English and French 1930–1978* (New York: Grove Press, 1977).

———. *The Collected Shorter Plays of Samuel Beckett* (New York: Grove Press, 1984).

———. *The Complete Short Prose, 1929–1989*, ed. S.E. Gontarski (New York: Grove Press, 1995).

———. *Company* (London: John Calder, 1980).

———. *Disjecta: Miscellaneous Writings and a Dramatic Fragment*, ed. Ruby Cohn (London: John Calder, 1983).

———. *Dream of Fair to Middling Women* (Dublin: Black Cat Press, 1992).

———. *Film* (New York: Grove Press, 1969).

———. *Happy Days* (New York: Grove Press, 1961).

———. *How It Is* (New York: Grove Press, 1964).

———. *Ill Seen Ill Said* (New York: Grove Press, 1981).

———. *'Krapp's Last Tape' and Other Dramatic Pieces* (New York: Grove Press, 1960).

———. *Malone Dies* (New York: Grove Press, 1956).

——. *Molloy* (New York: Grove Press, 1955).

——. *More Pricks Than Kicks* (London: Calder & Boyars, 1970).

——. *Murphy* (New York: Grove Press, 1958).

——. *Proust* (New York: Grove Press [first published 1931]).

——. *Stories and Texts for Nothing* (New York: Grove Press, 1967).

——. *The Unnamable* (New York: Grove Press, 1958).

——. *Watt* (New York: Grove Press, 1959).

——. *Worstward Ho* (New York: Grove Press, 1983).

Begam, Richard. *Samuel Beckett and the End of Modernity* (Stanford: Stanford University Press, 1996).

Benedikt, Michael and George E. Wellwarth, eds. and trans. *Modern French Theatre: The Avant Garde, Dada and Surrealism* (New York: Dutton, 1966).

Ben-Zvi, Linda and Angela Moorjani, eds. *Beckett at 100: Revolving It All* (New York: Oxford University Press, 2008).

Berry, Cicely, *The Actor and His Text* (London: Harrap, 1973).

Brandreth, Gyles. *John Gielgud: An Actor's Life*, 2nd edn. (London: Sutton, 2001).

Brater, Enoch. *Arthur Miller: A Playwright's Life and Works* (London: Thames & Hudson, 2005).

——. *Beyond Minimalism: Beckett's Late Style in the Theater* (New York: Oxford University Press, 1987).

——. *The Drama in the Text: Beckett's Late Fiction* (New York: Oxford University Press, 1994).

——. *The Essential Samuel Beckett* (London: Thames & Hudson, 2003).

——. *Why Beckett* (London: Thames & Hudson, 1989).

——, ed. *Arthur Miller: Death of a Salesman* (London: Methuen Drama, 2010).

——, ed. *Beckett at 80/Beckett in Context* (New York: Oxford University Press, 1986).

—— and Ruby Cohn, eds. *Around the Absurd: Essays on Modern and Postmodern Drama* (Ann Arbor: University of Michigan Press, 1990).

Brienza, Susan D. *Samuel Beckett's New Worlds: Style in Metafiction* (Norman: University of Oklahoma Press, 1987).

Brook, Peter. *The Empty Space* (New York: Atheneum, 1987).

Brooks, Cleanth. *The Well Wrought Urn: Studies in the Structure of Poetry* (New York; Harcourt, Brace & World, 1947).

Bryden, Mary, ed. *Samuel Beckett and Music* (Oxford: Oxford University Press, 1998).

Cage, John. *Silence: Lectures and Writings* (Middletown: Wesleyan University Press, 1961).

Calder, John, ed. *Beckett at Sixty* (London: Calder & Boyars, 1967).

Caselli, Daniela. *Beckett's Dantes: Intertextuality in the Fiction and Criticism* (Manchester: Manchester University Press, 2005).

——, ed. *Beckett and Nothing: Trying to Understand Beckett* (Manchester: Manchester University Press, 2010).

Chekhov, Anton. *The Plays of Anton Chekhov*, trans. Paul Schmidt (New York: HarperCollins, 1999).

Cohn, Ruby. *From* Desire *to* Godot: *Pocket Theater of Postwar Paris* (Berkeley: University of California Press, 1987).

——. *Just Play: Beckett's Theater* (Princeton: Princeton University Press, 1980).

Cronin, Anthony. *Samuel Beckett: The Last Modernist* (New York: HarperCollins, 1997).

Dante Aligheri. *The Inferno*, trans. J.A. Carlyle, rev. by H. Oelsner (London: J.M. Dent, 1932).

Dickerman, Leah, ed. *Dada: Zurich, Berlin, Hannover, Cologne, New York, Paris* (Washington, D.C.: National Gallery of Art/DAP, 2006).

Duckworth, Colin. *Angels of Darkness: Dramatic Effect in Beckett and Ionesco* (London: Allen & Unwin, 1972).

Elam, Keir. *The Semiotics of Theatre and Drama* (London: Methuen, 1980).

Eliot, T.S. *The Complete Poems of T.S. Eliot* (London: Faber & Faber, 1969).

Ellmann, Richard. *James Joyce* (New York: Oxford University Press, 1959).

Esslin, Martin. *Mediations: Essays on Brecht, Beckett, and the Media* (Baton Rouge: Louisiana State University Press, 1980).

——. *The Theatre of the Absurd* (Garden City, NY: Anchor, 1961).

Fehsenfeld, Martha Dow and Lois More Overbeck, eds. *The Letters of Samuel Beckett*, vol. 1: *1929–1940* (Cambridge: Cambridge University Press, 2009).

Fischer-Dieskau, Dietrich. *The Fischer-Dieskau Book of Lieder*, trans. George Bird and Richard Stokes (New York: Limelight, 1984).

Frenz, Horst, ed. *American Playwrights on Drama* (New York: Hill & Wang, 1965).

Fuchs, Elinor and Una Chaudhuri, eds. *Land/Scape/Theater* (Ann Arbor: University of Michigan Press, 2002).

Garner, Stanton B., Jr. *Phenomenology and Performance in Contemporary Drama* (Ithaca: Cornell University Press, 1994).

Geis, Deborah R. *Postmodern Theatric[ks]: Monologue in Contemporary American Drama* (Ann Arbor: University of Michigan Press, 1993).

Goodman, Randolph, ed. *From Script to Stage: Eight Modern Plays* (San Francisco: Rinehart Press, 1971).

Graver, Lawrence and Raymond Federman, eds. *Samuel Beckett: The Critical Heritage* (London: Routledge & Kegan Paul, 1979).

Harmon, Maurice, ed. *No Author Better Served: The Correspondence of Samuel Beckett and Alan Schneider* (Cambridge, MA: Harvard University Press, 1998).

Harvey, Lawrence E. *Samuel Beckett: Poet and Critic* (Princeton: Princeton University Press, 1970).

Hutcheon, Linda. *A Poetics of Postmodernism: History, Theory, Fiction* (London: Routledge, 1987).

Ibsen, Henrik. *Four Major Plays*, vol. 1, trans. Rolf Fjelde (New York: Signet, 1992, repr. 2006); vol. 2 (New York: Signet, 2001).

Jameson, Frederic. *Postmodernism: The Cultural Logic of Late Capitalism* (Durham: Duke University Press, 1991).

Joyce, James. *Ulysses* (New York: Modern Library, 1961).

Knowlson, James. *Damned to Fame: The Life of Samuel Beckett* (New York: Simon & Schuster, 1996).

——. *Light and Darkness in the Theatre of Samuel Beckett* (London: Turret Books, 1972).

——, ed. *The Theatrical Notebooks of Samuel Beckett*, vol. 3: *Krapp's Last Tape* (London: Faber & Faber, 1992).

Krance, Charles, ed. *Samuel Beckett's 'Company/Compagnie' and 'A Piece of Monologue/Solo': A Bilingual Variorum Edition* (New York: Garland, 1993).

Kushner, Tony. *Angels in America* (New York: Theater Communications Group, 1993).

McFarlane, James, ed. *The Cambridge Companion to Ibsen* (Cambridge: Cambridge University Press, 1994).

Martin, Robert A. and Steven R. Centola, eds. *The Theater Essays of Arthur Miller* (New York: Da Capo Press, 1996).

Mason, Ellsworth and Richard Ellmann, eds. *The Critical Writings of James Joyce* (London: Faber & Faber, 1959).

Meyer, Michael. *Ibsen: A Biography* (New York: Doubleday, 1971).

Miller, Arthur. *Arthur Miller Plays: Two* (London: Methuen Drama, 2009).

——. *Death of a Salesman* (New York: Viking, 1958).

——. *Timebends: A Life* (New York: Grove Press, 1987).

Motherwell, Robert, ed. *The Dada Painters and Poets* (Cambridge: Harvard University Press, 2005).

Nixon, Mark and Matthew Feldman, eds. *The International Reception of Samuel Beckett* (London: Continuum, 2009).

Ondaatje, Michael. *Divisadero* (New York: Knopf, 2007).

Oppenheim, Lois. *Directing Beckett* (Ann Arbor: University of Michigan Press, 1994).

——. *The Painted Word: Samuel Beckett's Dialogue with Art* (Ann Arbor: University of Michigan Press, 2000).

——, ed. *Palgrave Advances in Samuel Beckett Studies* (Basingstoke: Palgrave Macmillan, 2004).

——, ed. *Samuel Beckett and the Arts: Music, Visual Arts, and Non-Print Media* (New York: Garland, 1999).

Our Exagmination Round His Factification for Incamination of Work in Progress (Paris: Shakespeare & Company, 1929).

Perkins, David, ed. *English Romantic Writers* (New York: Harcourt, Brace & World, 1967).

Perloff, Marjorie, ed. *Postmodern Genres* (Norman: University of Oklahoma Press, 1988).

Pilling, John, ed. *The Cambridge Companion to Samuel Beckett* (Cambridge: Cambridge University Press, 1994).

Pinter, Harold. *The Homecoming* (New York: Grove Press, 1967).

——. *No Man's Land* (New York: Grove Press, 1975).

Rabaté, Jean-Michel. *The Ghosts of Modernism* (Gainesville: University of Florida Press, 1996).

Raynor, Alice. *To Act, to Do, to Perform: Drama and the Phenomenology of Action* (Ann Arbor: University of Michigan Press, 1994).

Rondeau, James and Douglas Druick, eds. *Jasper Johns GRAY* (New Haven: Yale University Press, 2007).

Rosenberg, Harold. *The Anxious Object: Art Today and Its Audience* (New York: Horizon, 1964).

Schneider, Alan. *Entrances: An American Director's Journey* (New York: Viking, 1986).

Schwitters, Kurt. *PPPPPP: Poems Performances Pieces Proses Plays Poetics*, ed. and trans. Jerome Rothenberg and Pierre Joris (Philadelphia: Temple Universiy Press, 1994).

Serpiere, Alessandro. *Come communica il teatro: dal testo alla scena* (Milan: Il Formichiere, 1978).

Shakespeare, William. *The Riverside Shakespeare*, 2nd edn. (Boston and New York: Houghton Mifflin, 1997).

Shaw, Bernard. *The Quintessence of Ibsenism* (New York: Hill & Wang, 1957).

Shroder, Maurice Z. *Poètes français du dix-neuvième siècle* (Cambridge, MA: Harvard University Press, 1964).

Sprinchorn, Evert. *Strindberg as Dramatist* (New Haven: Yale University Press, 1982).

States, Bert O. *Great Reckonings in Little Rooms: On the Phenomenology of Theater* (Berkeley: University of California Press, 1985).

Stoppard, Tom. *The Coast of Utopia* (New York: Grove Press, 2002).

——. *Jumpers* (New York: Grove Press, 1972).

——. *The Real Inspector Hound* (New York: Grove Press, 1969).

——. *Rosencrantz and Guildenstern Are Dead* (New York: Grove Press, 1967).

Strindberg, August. *A Dream Play* in *Six Plays of Strindberg*, trans. Elizabeth Sprigge (New York: Doubleday, 1955).

van Hulle, Dirk. *Beckett the European* (Tallahassee: Journal of Beckett Studies Books, 2005).

Virgil. *The Aeneid*, trans. Robert Fitzgerald (New York: Vintage, 1990).

von der Vogelweide, Walter. *'I Saw the World': Sixty Poems from Walther von der Vogelweide, 1170–1228*, trans. Ian G. Colvin (London: Edward Arnold, 1938).

Whitelaw, Billie. *Billie Whitelaw: . . . Who He?* (New York: St. Martin's Press, 1995).

Willett, John, ed. *Brecht on Theatre* (New York: Hill & Wang, 1964).

Williams, Tennessee. *A Streetcar Named Desire* (New York: Signet, 1974).

Yeats, William Butler. *The Collected Plays of W.B. Yeats* (New York: Macmillan, 1953).

——. *The Collected Poems of W.B. Yeats* (New York: Macmillan, 1956).

NOTES

Notes to Preface

1. Samuel Beckett, *Molloy* (New York: Grove Press, 1955), p. 226. For the poem by John Keats, see the first line of *Endymion*, Book 1, in *English Romantic Writers*, ed. David Perkins (New York: Harcourt, Brace & World, 1967), p. 1137.
2. See Enoch Brater, *Why Beckett* (London: Thames & Hudson, 1989), p. 68.
3. Samuel Beckett, 'Whoroscope', in *Collected Poems 1930–1978* (London: John Calder, 1986), p. 1.
4. Samuel Beckett, *The Unnamable* (New York: Grove Press, 1958), p. 3; *Molloy*, p. 41; Samuel Beckett, '*Intercessions* by Denis Devlin', in *Disjecta: Miscellaneous Writings and a Dramatic Fragment*, ed. Ruby Cohn (London: John Calder, 1983), p. 91; *The Inferno of Dante Aligheri*, trans. J.A. Carlyle, rev. by H. Oelsner (London: J.M. Dent, 1932), canto IX, 1, 130, pp. 98–9; Samuel Beckett, *Ohio Impromptu*, in *The Collected Shorter Plays of Samuel Beckett* (New York: Grove Press, 1984), p. 288.
5. Alan Schneider quoted by Ruby Cohn in 'Growing (Up?) with *Godot*', in *Beckett at 80/Beckett in Context*, ed. Enoch Brater (New York: Oxford University Press, 1986), p. 13; *Molloy*, p. 147; Samuel Beckett, *Worstward Ho* (New York: Grove Press, 1983), p. 7.

Notes to Chapter 1

1. Citations from *Waiting for Godot* in my text are from the Grove Press edition (New York, 1954).
2. For background information concerning the composition of this play and the history and reception of its productions in Europe and America, see in particular James Knowlson, *Damned to Fame: The Life of Samuel Beckett* (New York: Simon & Schuster, 1996); Ruby Cohn, *From Desire to Godot: Pocket Theater of Postwar Paris* (Berkeley: University of California Press, 1987); Alan Schneider, *Entrances: An American Director's Journey* (New York: Viking, 1986); and Enoch Brater, *The Essential Samuel Beckett* (London: Thames & Hudson, 2003).
3. Beckett quoted in Brater, *The Essential Samuel Beckett*, p. 55.
4. *The Essential Samuel Beckett*, pp. 10, 82.
5. Ibid., p. 65. See also *The Letters of Samuel Beckett*, vol. 1: *1929–1940*, ed. Martha Dow Fehsenfeld and Lois More Overbeck (Cambridge: Cambridge University Press, 2009), pp. 150, 257.
6. Samuel Beckett, *Proust* (New York: Grove Press, [first published 1931]), p. 3.

7. Samuel Beckett, 'Dante . . . Bruno. Vico . . Joyce', in *Our Exagmination Round His Factification for Incamination of Work in Progress* (Paris: Shakespeare & Company, 1929), p. 22.

8. Tom Stoppard, *Jumpers* (New York: Grove Press, 1972), p. 28.

9. Personal communication to the author; *The Essential Samuel Beckett*, p. 75.

10. Ibid.

11. Samuel Beckett, 'From an Abandoned Work', in *The Complete Short Prose, 1929–1989*, ed. S.E. Gontarski (New York: Grove Press, 1995), p. 158.

12. Samuel Beckett, 'Gnome', in *Collected Poems in English and French 1930–1978* (New York: Grove Press, 1977), p. 7.

13. For an account of Beckett's actions in France during the Second World War, see Knowlson, *Damned to Fame,* pp. 273–308.

14. Ibid.

15. Ibid.

16 Schneider, quoted by Cohn, see note 5 for Preface, p. 169.

17. Tom Driver, 'Beckett by the Madeleine', in *Columbia University Forum* 4 (1961), 23; and H. Porter Abbott, '"I Am Not a Philosopher"', in *Beckett at 100: Revolving It All*, ed. Linda Ben-Zvi and Angela Moorjani (New York: Oxford University Press, 2008), pp. 81–92. Morton Feldman's comments on Beckett as 'a fifties writer' can be found on the tape for *Words and Music* (1987) in the American Beckett Festival of Radio Plays, directed by Everett Frost.

18. Martin Esslin, *The Theatre of the Absurd* (Garden City, NY: Anchor, 1961).

19. Knowlson, *Damned to Fame,* pp. 261–2.

20. Ibid., p. 98.

21. Ibid., pp. 59–64.

22. Ibid., p. 47. For Beckett's earlier unease with writing in English, see *The Letters of Samuel Beckett*, vol. 1, p. 205: 'No sooner do I take up my pen to compose something in English than I get the feeling of being "de-personified".'

23. See the bilingual edition of the play published by Grove Press (New York, 2006); and Hersh Zeifman, 'The Alterable Whey of Words: The Texts of *Waiting for Godot*', in *Educational Theatre Journal* (1977), pp. 77–84.

24. Schneider, *Entrances*, pp. 221–39; see also *No Author Better Served: The Correspondence of Samuel Beckett and Alan Schneider*, ed. Maurice Harmon (Cambridge, MA: Harvard University Press, 1998).

25. For a discussion of this issue from a variety of critical perspectives, see *Beckett and Nothing: Trying to Understand Beckett*, ed. Daniela Caselli (Manchester: Manchester University Press, 2010).

26. Publicity materials for the 2009 London production of *Waiting for Godot*.

27. The first scholarly article published on *Waiting for Godot* was Edith Kern's 'Drama Stripped for Inaction: Beckett's *Godot*', in *Yale French Studies* 14 (1954–55), pp. 41–7.

28. Publicity materials for the 2009 London production of *Waiting for Godot*; see also *Jumpers*, p. 89.

29. See *The International Reception of Samuel Beckett*, ed. Mark Nixon and Matthew Feldman (London: Continuum, 2009); and Enoch Brater, 'The Globalization of Beckett's *Godot*', in *Comparative Drama* 37 (Summer 2003), pp. 145–58.

30. Erika Munk, 'Notes from a Trip to Sarajevo', in *Theater* 24 (1993), pp. 31–6.

31. *The Theatrical Notebooks of Samuel Beckett*, vol. 1: *Waiting for Godot*, ed. Dougald McMillan and James Knowlson (New York: Grove Press, 1993).

32. Beckett quoted in *The Essential Samuel Beckett*, p. 75.

Notes to Chapter 2

1. See Robert Motherwell, ed., *The Dada Painters and Poets* (Cambridge: Harvard University Press, 2005), p. 92.

2. Kurt Schwitters, *PPPPPP: Poems Performances Pieces Proses Plays Poetics*, ed. and trans. Jerome Rothenberg and Pierre Joris (Philadelphia: Temple University Press, 1994), p. 215.

3. See Susan D. Brienza, *Samuel Beckett's New Worlds: Style in Metafiction* (Norman: University of Oklahoma Press, 1987), pp. 179–96.

4. See Martin Esslin, 'Samuel Beckett – Infinity, Eternity', in *Beckett at 80/ Beckett in Context*, ed. Brater, pp. 117–20; and Enoch Brater, *The Drama in the Text: Beckett's Late Fiction* (New York: Oxford University Press, 1994), pp. 90–9.

5. See S.E. Gontarski, ' "Making Yourself All Up Again": The Composition of Samuel Beckett's *That Time*', in *Modern Drama* (June 1980), p. 112.

6. See *Modern French Theatre: The Avant Garde, Dada, and Surrealism*, ed. and trans. Michael Benedikt and George E. Wellwarth (New York: Dutton, 1966), p. xxxi.

7. See *Dada: Zurich, Berlin, Hannover, Cologne, New York, Paris*, ed. Leah Dickerman (Washington, D.C.: National Gallery of Art/DAP, 2006); and Charles Simic, 'Making It New', in *The New York Review of Books* (10 August 2006), pp. 10–13.

8. See Motherwell, pp. 81–2.

9. See Enoch Brater, *Beyond Minimalism: Beckett's Late Style in the Theater* (New York: Oxford University Press, 1987), p. 10.

10 See *No Author Better Served*, p. 24.

11. See Knowlson, *Damned to Fame*, p. 128.

12. For a careful examination of such 'demented particulars', see C.J. Ackerley, *Demented Particulars: The Annotated Murphy* (Tallahassee: Journal of Beckett Studies Books, 1998). For studies of Beckett in relation to other artists, see *Samuel Beckett and the Arts: Music, Visual Arts, and Non-Print Media*, ed. Lois Oppenheim (New York: Garland, 1999); *Samuel Beckett and Music*, ed. Mary Bryden (Oxford: Oxford University Press, 1998); and Lois Oppenheim, *The Painted Word: Samuel Beckett's Dialogue with Art* (Ann Arbor: University of Michigan Press, 2000). Daniel Albright in *Beckett and Aesthetics* (Cambridge:

Cambridge University Press, 2003) tries to make the case that surrealism is central to any understanding of Beckett's work. His *Representation and the Imagination: Beckett, Kafka, Nabokov, and Schoenberg* (Chicago: University of Chicago Press, 1981) is far more successful in positioning Beckett in relation to his time.

13. Driver, pp. 22–3.
14. See Alan Schneider, 'Waiting for Beckett', in *Beckett at Sixty*, ed. John Calder (London: Calder & Boyars, 1967), p. 34.
15. See, for example, Knowlson, *Damned to Fame*, pp. 504, 520–2, 533, 601–2; and *The Letters of Samuel Beckett*, vol. 1, pp. 68–9.

Notes to Chapter 3

1. Citations in my text from *Waiting for Godot* are from the Grove Press edition.
2. For Peter Brook's work with the RSC, see Sally Beauman, *The Royal Shakespeare Company: A History of Ten Decades* (Oxford: Oxford University Press, 1982); see also Peter Brook, *The Empty Space* (New York: Atheneum, 1987). On the question of stage landscape, see the essays collected in *Land/Scape/Theater*, ed. Elinor Fuchs and Una Chaudhuri (Ann Arbor: University of Michigan Press, 2002).
3. Brater, *Why Beckett*, p. 62.
4. Walter Asmus commented on *Godot* when he participated in the panel on 'Beckett and Performance II', part of the Beckett Centenary Symposium at Trinity College Dublin, 8 April 2006.
5. Alan Schneider often used this phrase in conversation when discussing the logistics of directing Beckett. See Alan Schneider, *Entrances: No Author Better Served*; and Lois Oppenheim, *Directing Beckett* (Ann Arbor: University of Michigan Press, 1994), pp. 315–18.
6. Cohn, *From Desire to Godot*, pp. 134 ff.
7. William Butler Yeats, *Purgatory*, in *The Collected Plays of W.B. Yeats* (New York: Macmillan, 1953), p. 430.
8. John Banville's comments during the round table discussion on 'Beckett and the Visual Arts', held at the National Gallery of Ireland, 9 April 2006.
9. For illustrations of designs by Giacometti and le Brocquy for *Waiting for Godot*, see Brater, *Why Beckett*, pp. 70, 72.
10. C.J. Ackerley and S.E. Gontarski, *The Grove Companion to Samuel Beckett* (New York: Grove Press, 2004), p. 329.
11. See, for example, Tom Stoppard, *The Real Inspector Hound* (New York: Grove Press, 1969).
12. Brater, *Why Beckett*, p. 73.
13. Beckett's uneasiness with the realistic techniques of Balzac is reflected in early works such as *Dream of Fair to Middling Women* and *More Pricks Than Kicks*;

his fascination with Proust is everywhere apparent in his monograph on the author (New York: Grove, 1957). See Knowlson, *Damned to Fame*.

14. See Bert O. States, *Great Reckonings in Little Rooms: On the Phenomenology of Theater* (Berkeley: University of California Press, 1985).

15. Citations from *Endgame* in my text are from the Grove Press edition (New York, 1958).

16. Citations from *Happy Days* in my text are from the Grove Press edition (New York: 1961).

17. Arthur Miller to this author, October 1981.

18. Knowlson, pp. 294–6.

19. Samuel Beckett, *Stories and Texts for Nothing* (New York: Grove Press, 1967), p. 96.

20. Beckett, *. . . but the clouds . . .* , in *The Collected Shorter Plays of Samuel Beckett*, p. 261.

21. Citations in this chapter from *Krapp's Last Tape* are from *'Krapp's Last Tape' and Other Dramatic Pieces* (New York: Grove Press, 1960).

22. See Brater, *Beyond Minimalism*, p. 93.

23. Jocelyn Herbert shared Beckett's advice to her about his late style in the theatre with this author in June 1997.

24. See Brater, *Beyond Minimalism*, pp. 18–36.

25. H. Porter Abbott, 'A Grammar for Being Elsewhere', *Journal of Modern Literature* (February 1977), pp. 39–46.

26. Samuel Beckett to this author, May 1976.

27. Jessica Tandy, who created the role of Mouth in the world premiere of *Not I* at Lincoln Center in New York in 1972, told this author in 1973 that Beckett was surprised by her question about whether or not the monologue alludes to a scene of rape in the field.

28. The dance critic John Rockwell has considered several of the same aesthetic questions in 'If It's Physical, It's Dance'; see the Arts Section of *The New York Times* (Sunday 12 March 2006), p. 9.

29. Brater, *Why Beckett*, p. 110.

30. *Othello*, I.iii.159. Citations from Shakespeare in the text are from *The Riverside Shakespeare*, 2nd edn. (Boston, New York: Houghton Mifflin, 1997).

31. Citations in my text from *Footfalls, Rockaby, Ohio Impromptu, What Where* and Beckett's television plays are from *The Collected Shorter Plays of Samuel Beckett*.

32. See Strindberg's Preface to *A Dream Play* in *Six Plays of Strindberg*, trans. Elizabeth Sprigge (New York: Doubleday, 1955), p. 193.

33. John Banville, *The Sea* (London: Picador, 2005), p. 129.

34. Samuel Beckett, *All That Fall* in *The Collected Shorter Plays of Samuel Beckett*, p. 23.

35. *Waiting for Godot*, p. 39.

36. Samuel Beckett, *Malone Dies* (New York: Grove Press, 1956), p. 108.

Notes to Chapter 4

1. All citations from Beckett's trilogy of novels, *Molloy*, *Malone Dies* and *The Unnamable* are taken in no particular order from their Grove Press editions. For additional uses of the word 'grey' in the trilogy, see Michèle Aina Barale and Rubin Rabinovitz, eds., *A KWIC Concordance to Samuel Beckett's Trilogy: 'Molloy', 'Malone Dies' and 'The Unnamable'*, vol. 1 (New York: Garland, 1988), pp. 361–2. *Jasper Johns GRAY*, ed. James Rondeau and Douglas Druick (New Haven: Yale University Press, 2007), discusses several of the issues raised in this chapter concerning Beckett's exploration of the colour grey.

2. Samuel Beckett, *Murphy* (New York: Grove Press, 1957), p. 1.

3. *Footfalls*, p. 242.

4. *Hamlet*, I.ii.240–1.

5. All citations in my text from *Waiting for Godot* are from the Grove Press edition.

6. See Brater, *The Essential Samuel Beckett*, p. 78.

7. Jessica Tandy, quoted by Brater in *Beyond Minimalism*, p. 4.

8. All citations in my text from *Endgame* are from the Grove Press edition.

9. All citations in this chapter from *Krapp's Last Tape* are taken from '*Krapp's Last Tape*' and Other Dramatic Pieces.

10. James Knowlson, *Light and Darkness in the Theatre of Samuel Beckett* (London: Turret Books, 1972). On variations of the colour grey, see in particular Jean-Michel Rabaté, *The Ghosts of Modernism* (Gainesville: University of Florida Press, 1996); and Roland Barthes, *A Lover's Discourse: Fragments*, trans. Richard Howard (New York: Hill & Wang, 1979).

11. *Proust*, p. 19. See also *The Letters of Samuel Beckett*, vol. 1, pp. 26, 46.

12. See James Knowlson, ed., *The Theatrical Notebooks of Samuel Beckett*, vol. 3: *Krapp's Last Tape* (London: Faber, 1992).

13. All citations in my text from *Happy Days* are from the Grove Press edition.

14. See the final line in 'The Circus Animals' Desertion' in *The Collected Poems of W.B. Yeats*, p. 336.

15. Beckett quoted by Brater, *The Essential Samuel Beckett*, p. 102.

16. Ibid., p. 104.

17. All citations in my text from *Film* are from the Grove Press edition.

18. See Knowlson, *Damned to Fame*, pp. 212–13; and Anthony Cronin, *Samuel Beckett: The Last Modernist* (New York: HarperCollins, 1997), p. 228.

19. Bruce Nauman quoted by James Rondeau, 'Jasper Johns: Gray', in *Jasper Johns GRAY*, p. 33. This monograph was published in coordination with a major exhibition of Johns's paintings at the Art Institute of Chicago (3 November 2007 to 6 January 2008) and at the Metropolitan Museum of Art in New York (5 February to 4 May 2008).

20. All citations in my text from Beckett's plays for television are from *The Collected Shorter Plays of Samuel Beckett*.

21. Samuel Beckett, *Company* (London: John Calder, 1980), p. 7.

22. All citations from Beckett's late plays are from *The Collected Shorter Plays of Samuel Beckett*.
23. Giacometti quoted by Rondeau, p. 45. The artist designed the tree in *En attendant Godot* for the 1961 Paris revival; see Brater, *The Essential Samuel Beckett*, pp. 66, 72.
24. Beckett quoted by Brater in *Beyond Minimalism*, p. 109.
25. See, for example, Beckett's comments to Billie Whitelaw concerning *Not I*, cited by Brater, *Beyond Minimalism*, p. 21.
26. Beckett quoted by Rondeau, in Rondeau and Druick, eds., p. 45.

Notes to Chapter 5

1. *Footfalls*, p. 243.
2. *Happy Days*, p. 37.
3. See Brater, *The Essential Samuel Beckett*, p. 107; and Samuel Beckett, *Not I*, in *The Collected Shorter Plays of Samuel Beckett*, p. 216.
4. Jessica Tandy, quoted by Brater in *Beyond Minimalism*, p. 4.
5. See Louis Menard, 'The Aesthete', *The New Yorker* (4 June 2007), pp. 92–4.
6. See Knowlson, *Damned to Fame*, p. 348; and Brater, *The Essential Samuel Beckett*, pp. 59–60.
7. Eugene O'Neill, 'Strindberg and Our Theatre', in *American Playwrights on Drama*, ed. Horst Frenz (New York: Hill & Wang, 1965), pp. 1–2.
8. Citations from *Macbeth* are from the second edition of *The Riverside Shakespeare*.
9. See Bernard Shaw, *The Quintessence of Ibsenism* (New York: Hill & Wang, 1957).
10. 'From Ibsen's Notes', in Randolph Goodman, ed., *From Script to Stage: Eight Modern Plays* (San Francisco: Rinehart Press, 1971), p. 43.
11. Citations from *Hedda Gabler* are taken from *Ibsen: Four Major Plays*, vol. 1, trans. Rolf Fjelde (New York: Signet, 1992).
12. All citations from *Uncle Vanya*, *Three Sisters* and *The Seagull* are from *The Plays of Anton Chekhov*, trans. Paul Schmidt (New York: HarperCollins, 1999).
13. *Hamlet*, II.2.
14. Harold Pinter, *No Man's Land* (New York: Grove Press, 1975), p. 95; *The Homecoming* (New York: Grove Press, 1967), p. 34.
15. Beckett, quoted by Brater in *The Essential Samuel Beckett*, p. 55.
16. For Beckett's interest in the visual arts, especially painting, see Knowlson, *Damned to Fame*; and Oppenheim, *The Painted Word*.
17. Citations in my text from *Endgame* are from the Grove Press edition.
18. Citations in my text from *Waiting for Godot* are from the Grove Press edition.
19. Ian G. Colvin, trans., *'I Saw the World': Sixty Poems from Walther von der Vogelweide, 1170–1228* (London: Edward Arnold, 1938), p. 49. See also Knowlson, *Damned to Fame*, pp. 147, 613.

20. *Malone Dies*, p. 62.

21. Beckett, quoted by Brater in *The Essential Samuel Beckett*, p. 78.

22. On the figure of Belacqua as he appears in Beckett's work, see Ackerley and Gontarski, pp. 46–8.

23. *Murphy*, p. 111.

24. See Alice Raynor, *To Act, to Do, to Perform: Drama and the Phenomenology of Action* (Ann Arbor: University of Michigan Press, 1994); and Stanton B. Garner, Jr., *Phenomenology and Performance in Contemporary Drama* (Ithaca: Cornell University Press, 1994).

25. All citations from *Krapp's Last Tape* in this chapter are from *The Collected Shorter Plays of Samuel Beckett*, pp. 55–63.

26. Dylan Thomas, writing about Beckett in the *New English Weekly* (17 March 1938). See Lawrence Graver and Raymond Federman, eds., *Samuel Beckett: The Critical Heritage* (London: Routledge & Kegan Paul, 1979), p. 46.

27. See Holland Cotter, 'Sonnets in Marble', *The New York Times* (10 August 1977), B25, 30.

28. Citations from *Come and Go* are taken from *The Collected Shorter Plays of Samuel Beckett*, pp. 194–5.

29. *Rockaby*, pp. 275–82. For the playwright's comments on this piece, see Brater, *Beyond Minimalism*, pp. 173–4.

30. Beckett, 'Dante . . . Bruno. Vico . . Joyce', p. 22.

31. *Ohio Impromptu*, pp. 285–8.

32. Charles Baudelaire, 'Au Lecture', in *Poètes français du dix-neuvième siècle*, ed. Maurice Z. Shroder (Cambridge, Mass.: Harvard University Press, 1964), p. 92.

33. *The Inferno of Dante Alighieri*, canto IX, 1, 130, pp. 98–9. For a detailed study of the Dante–Beckett connection, see Daniela Caselli, *Beckett's Dantes: Intertextuality in the Fiction and Criticism* (Manchester: Manchester University Press, 2005).

34. Nabokov quoted by Michael Ondaatje in *Divisadero* (New York: Knopf, 2007), p. 136.

35. *The Unnamable*, p. 33.

Notes to Chapter 6

1. For useful perspectives related to the point of this discussion, see in particular Lionel Abel, *Metatheatre: A New View of Dramatic Form* (New York: Hill & Wang, 1963); and John Willett, ed., *Brecht on Theatre* (New York: Hill & Wang, 1964).

2. The Italian actress Isa Danieli made effective use of this 'alienation' device in Cristina Pezzoli's 2009–2010 production of *Mother Courage* for Gli Ipocriti, the theatre company based in Naples.

3. See the Prologue to *Henry V*; *The Tempest*, IV.i.148–58; and *Hamlet*, II.ii.301.

4. A 'Mr. Beckett' also figures in the author's *Dream of Fair to Middling Women* (Dublin: Black Cat Press, 1992), pp. 69, 141, 186.

5. See Goodman, pp. 206–7.

6. Citations in the text from *Waiting for Godot* are from the Grove Press edition.

7. *The Unnamable*, p. 83.

8. See S.E. Gontarski, '"Making Yourself All Up Again": The Composition of Beckett's *That Time*', in *Modern Drama* 23 (June 1980), p. 112.

9. Citatons in the text from *Endgame* are from the Grove Press edition.

10. Citations in the text from *All That Fall* are from *The Collected Shorter Plays of Samuel Beckett*.

11. *Murphy*, p. 122; *The Unnamable*, p. 85.

12. Samuel Beckett, *Watt* (New York: Grove Press, 1959), p. 237.

13. Quoted by Colin Duckworth in *Angels of Darkness: Dramatic Effect in Beckett and Ionesco* (London: Allen & Unwin, 1972), p. 68.

14. See Brater, *Beyond Minimalism*, p. 133.

15. Quoted by Brater in *The Essential Samuel Beckett*, p. 75.

16. Citations in this chapter from *Krapp's Last Tape* are from *'Krapp's Last Tape' and Other Dramatic Pieces*.

17. Beckett quoted in Brater, *The Essential Samuel Beckett*, p. 102; 'Gnome', in *Collected Poems in English and French, 1930–1978*, p. 7.

18. Brater, *The Essential Samuel Beckett*, p. 102.

19. Beckett's stage directions for *Happy Days*, p. 7.

20. All citations in the text from Beckett's shorter plays, including his scripts written for television, are from *The Collected Shorter Plays of Samuel Beckett*.

21. See Billie Whitelaw, *Billie Whitelaw: . . . Who He?* (New York: St. Martin's Press, 1995).

22. Schneider, *Entrances*, p. 269.

23. *Macbeth*, II.ii.24–9.

24. See Brater, *Beyond Minimalism*, p. 57.

25. Ibid., p. 126.

26. Ibid., pp. 126, 132.

27. Ibid., p. 173.

28. Billie Whitelaw in the film of *Rockaby* made by D.A. Pennebaker and Chris Hegedus (1984); see Brater, *Beyond Minimalism,* p. 174.

29. See Enoch Brater, 'Intertextuality', in *Palgrave Advances in Samuel Beckett Studies*, ed. Lois Oppenheim (Basingstoke: Palgrave Macmillan, 2004), pp. 30–44.

30. See the advice to the Players in *Hamlet*, III.ii.1.

31. Beckett's familiarity with Italian Renaissance painting is reflected most strongly in *The Letters of Samuel Beckett*, vol. 1; and in Knowlson, *Damned to Fame*.

32. *The Letters of Samuel Beckett*, vol. 1, p. 421.

33. Pirandello's play *Questa sera si recita a soggetto* (1928–9) is generally translated into English as *Tonight We Improvise*.

Notes to Chapter 7

1. Beckett quoted by Lawrence E. Harvey, *Samuel Beckett: Poet and Critic* (Princeton: Princeton University Press, 1970), p. 273.

2. Samuel Beckett, 'Walking Out', in *More Pricks Than Kicks* (London: Calder & Boyars, 1970), p. 114.

3. *Murphy*, pp. 8, 20, 106.

4. *Molloy*, p. 226.

5. See Ackerley and Gontarski, p. 487; and Philip Lauback-Kiani, ' "I Close My Eyes and Try and Imagine Them": Romantic Discourse Formations in *Krapp's Last Tape*', in *Beckett the European* (Tallahassee: Journal of Beckett Studies Books, 2005), pp. 125–36; *The Letters of Samuel Beckett*, p. 21. For 'profounds of mind', see *Ohio Impromptu*, p. 288.

6. *The Collected Letters of Samuel Beckett*, vol. 1, p. 108.

7. *Watt*, p. 246. For useful discussions relating to this point, see Eyal Amiran, *Wandering and Home: Beckett's Metaphysical Narrative* (University Park: Pennsylvania State University Press, 1993); and Richard Begam, *Samuel Beckett and the End of Modernity* (Stanford: Stanford University Press, 1996).

8. *The Unnamable*, p. 179.

9. See the last line of Tennyson's 'Ulysses' (1833) in *Major British Writers*, vol. 2, ed. G.B. Harrison (New York: Harcourt, Brace & World, 1959), p. 395.

10. See Tim Parks, 'Beckett: Still Stirring', in *The New York Review of Books*, 13 July 2006, p. 24.

11. *Molloy*, p. 112.

12. *The Unnamable*, p. 20.

13. *Malone Dies*, p. 98.

14. Ibid.

15. On the question of the 'voice verbatim', see Charles Krance, ed., *Samuel Beckett's 'Company/Compagnie' and 'A Piece of Monologue/Solo': A Bilingual Variorum Edition* (New York: Garland, 1993).

16. *Company*, pp. 12–13.

17. Ibid., pp. 11, 64.

18. Ibid., pp. 23–4.

19. Samuel Beckett, *Ill Seen Ill Said* (New York: Grove Press, 1981), p. 40. See also *The Collected Letters of Samuel Beckett*, vol. 1, p. 392.

20. *Worstward Ho*, pp. 43, 47. John Banville's narrator, part spy, part art historian, makes his own point about meaning vs. significance in *The Untouchable* (New York: Vintage, 1998), p. 312.

21. Samuel Beckett, *Film*, in *The Collected Shorter Plays of Samuel Beckett*, p. 169.

22. For Keats, see note 1 for Preface, p. 169.

23. *'Krapp's Last Tape' and Other Dramatic Pieces*, pp. 22–3, 27.

24. Knowlson, *Damned to Fame*, pp. 318–19.

25. See Bernard Beckerman, 'Beckett and the Act of Listening', in *Beckett at 80/ Beckett in Context*, ed. Brater.

26. Samuel Beckett, *Rough for Radio II*, in *The Collected Shorter Plays of Samuel Beckett*, p. 115.

27. W.B. Yeats, 'The Tower', in *The Collected Poems of W.B. Yeats*, p. 195.

28. *Macbeth*, V.v.43.

29. See William Wordsworth, 'Ode: Intimations of Immortality from Recollections of Early Childhood', in *English Romantic Writers*, ed. Perkins, p. 282.

30. See Schneider, *Entrances*, p. 269.

31. See Brater, *Beyond Minimalism*, pp. 107, 109, 160–4.

32. Samuel Beckett, *Ghost Trio*, in *The Collected Shorter Plays of Samuel Beckett*, p. 248.

33. See Samuel Beckett, 'Stirrings Still', in *Samuel Beckett: The Complete Short Prose*, p. 265; and *Endgame*, p. 81.

34. *Malone Dies*, p. 93; and *Footfalls*, p. 242.

35. Samuel Beckett, 'Ping', in *The Complete Short Prose*, p. 193.

Notes to Chapter 8

1. *Endgame*, p. 32; and *The Unnamable*, p. 110.

2. Samuel Beckett, *How It Is* (New York: Grove Press, 1964), p. 26.

3. Samuel Beckett, *A Piece of Monologue*, in *The Collected Shorter Plays of Samuel Beckett*, p. 268.

4. *Footfalls*, pp. 240–3.

5. See Richard Begam, *Samuel Beckett and the End of Modernity*; and H. Porter Abbott, 'Late Modernism: Samuel Beckett and the Art of the Oeuvre', in *Around the Absurd: Essays on Modern and Postmodern Drama*, ed. Enoch Brater and Ruby Cohn (Ann Arbor: University of Michigan Press, 1990), pp. 73–96. See also John Cage, *Silence: Lectures and Writings* (Middletown: Wesleyan University Press, 1961).

6. Samuel Beckett, *Play*, in *Collected Shorter Plays*, p. 156.

7. Citations in this chapter from *Krapp's Last Tape* are taken from *'Krapp's Last Tape' and Other Dramatic Pieces*.

8. *Waiting for Godot*, p. 8a.

9. *Murphy*, p. 148.

10. *Stories and Texts for Nothing*, p. 139.

11. *Watt*, p. 247.

12. See Samuel Beckett, *Disjecta*, pp. 51–4, 170–3.

13. *. . . but the clouds . . .*, p. 261; and *Watt*, p. 147.

14. For the 'unsaid' and the 'ununsaid', see in particular *Ill Seen Ill Said*; and *Worstward Ho*. See also *Watt*, p. 101.

15. See Caselli, *Beckett's Dantes*.

16. *The Unnamable*, p. 179.

17. See Brater, *The Essential Samuel Beckett*, p. 55.

18. *Watt*, p. 237. *Molloy*, *Malone Dies* and *The Unnamable*, read by Barry McGovern, were recorded in their entirety and produced for RTE Radio in 2006 by Tim Lehane at The Base, Dublin.

19. For the numerous adjectives modifying 'silence' in the trilogy, see *A KWIC Concordance to Samuel Beckett's Trilogy: 'Molloy', 'Malone Dies', and 'The Unnamable'*, vol. 2, pp. 830–3.

20. *Molloy*, p. 41; and *Ill Seen Ill Said*, for example, p. 48.

21. *Stories and Texts for Nothing*, p. 118.

22. *What Where*, p. 316.

23. See Cicely Berry, *The Actor and His Text* (London: Harrap, 1973).

24. *Stories and Texts for Nothing*, p. 104.

25. Ibid.

26. *The Unnamable*, p. 20; *Waiting for Godot*, p. 55b.

27. See *The Theatrical Notebooks of Samuel Beckett*, vols. 1–4, gen. ed. James Knowlson (London: Faber & Faber, 1993–99). See also Knowlson's *'Happy Days': Samuel Beckett's Production Notebook* (New York: Grove Press, 1985).

28. *Rockaby*, pp. 275–80.

29. *. . . but the clouds . . .* , p. 261.

30. *Stories and Texts for Nothing*, p. 139.

31. *Film*, pp. 163, 165.

32. *Ghost Trio*, in *Collected Shorter Plays*, p. 248.

33. *. . . but the clouds . . .* , p. 261.

34. See Brater, *Beyond Minimalism*, p. 93.

35. See Knowlson, *Damned to Fame*, pp. 385–7, 421, 442–3; and Martin Esslin, *Mediations: Essays on Brecht, Beckett, and the Media* (Baton Rouge: Louisiana State University Press, 1980), pp. 125–54. See also Beckerman, pp. 149–67.

36. *All That Fall*, p. 13.

37. Samuel Beckett, *Cascando* and *Rough for Radio I*, in *The Collected Shorter Plays of Samuel Beckett*, pp. 107, 137.

38. Quoted by Brater, *Beyond Minimalism*, p. 5.

39. See *Stories and Texts for Nothing*, p. 55; and *All That Fall*, p. 23. For a discussion of this point, see Brater, *The Drama in the Text*.

40. *Ill Seen Ill Said*, p. 7.

41. William Wordsworth, *The Prelude*, Book 1, lines 369–71; see *English Romantic Writers*, p. 217.

42. *Murphy*, p. 106.

43. A 'dud mystic' is the term Belacqua uses to announce the presence of a fictional 'Mr Beckett'. He 'meant *mystique raté*, but shrank always from the *mot juste*'. See Beckett, *Dream of Fair to Middling Women*, p. 186.

44. *Malone Dies*, p. 51; and *As the Story Was Told* (London: John Calder, 1990), pp. 131–4.

Notes to Chapter 9

1. Beckett, quoted in Brater, *The Essential Samuel Beckett*, p. 107. See also Errol Durbach, 'Afterword: Ibsen, Beckett, and Uncertainty', in *Modern Drama* (Fall 2006), pp. 396–401.
2. 'Ping', p. 193.
3. Michael Meyer, *Ibsen: A Biography* (New York: Doubleday, 1971), pp. 740–5.
4. See Bert O. States, *Great Reckonings in Little Rooms: On the Phenomenology of Theater* (Berkeley: University of California Press, 1985).
5. Citations in this chapter from the plays of Henrik Ibsen are from the English translations by Rolf Fjelde published in the centennial edition, *Ibsen: Four Major Plays*, vol. 1 (New York: Signet, 2006); and *Ibsen: Four Major Plays*, vol. 2 (New York: Signet, 2001).
6. T.S. Eliot, 'Burnt Norton', in *The Complete Poems of T.S. Eliot* (London: Faber & Faber, 1969), p. 171.
7. Evert Sprinchorn, *Strindberg as Dramatist* (New Haven: Yale University Press, 1982), p. 231. For the question of 'location' in *John Gabriel Borkman*, see Inga-Stina Ewbank, 'The Last Plays', in *The Cambridge Companion to Ibsen*, ed. James McFarlane (Cambridge: Cambridge University Press, 1994), pp. 147–50.
8. Unless otherwise noted, all citations in this chapter from the plays of Samuel Beckett are from *The Collected Shorter Plays of Samuel Beckett*.
9. See Brater, *The Essential Samuel Beckett*, p. 98.
10. For the Ibsen–Joyce connection, see Richard Ellmann, *James Joyce* (New York: Oxford University Press, 1959), pp. 72–82, 89–93. See also *The Critical Writings of James Joyce*, ed. Ellsworth Mason and Richard Ellmann (London: Faber & Faber, 1959).
11. *No Author Better Served*, pp. 285, 396, 466.
12. Cronin, p. 183.
13. Knowlson, *Damned to Fame*, p. 330.
14. *Endgame*, pp. 18, 50.
15. James Joyce, *Ulysses* (New York: Random House, 1986), pp. 715–16.
16. See Dietrich Fischer-Dieskau, *The Fischer-Dieskau Book of Lieder*, trans. George Bird and Richard Stokes (New York: Limelight, 1984), p. 303.

Notes to Chapter 10

1. Citations in the text from *Death of a Salesman* are from the Viking edition (New York, 1958). For background information concerning the history of this play in production, see Enoch Brater, *Arthur Miller: A Playwright's Life and Works* (London: Thames & Hudson, 2005), pp. 42–51.
2. Personal communication from the playwright, October 1981.
3. See Arthur Miller, 'Tragedy and the Common Man', in *The Theater Essays of Arthur Miller*, ed. Robert A. Martin and Steven R. Centola (New York: Da

Capo Press, 1996), pp. 3–7; and *Arthur Miller: Death of a Salesman,* ed. Enoch Brater (London: Methuen Drama, 2010), p. xliii.

4. See Alessandro Serpieri, *Come communica il teatro: dal testo alla scena* (Milan: Il Formichiere, 1978); and Keir Elam, *The Semiotics of Theatre and Drama* (London: Methuen, 1980).

5. Samuel Beckett, 'what is the word', in *As the Story Was Told: Uncollected and Late Prose* (London: John Calder, 1990), p. 132.

6. See Goodman, pp. 238–40; and Gyles Brandreth, *John Gielgud: An Actor's Life*, 2nd ed. (London: Sutton, 2001).

7. *Watt*, p. 254.

8. *Macbeth*, II.ii.33–41.

9. This famous line from Marianne Moore is from her first version of 'Poetry', heavily edited and pared down as it appears in *The Complete Poems of Marianne Moore* (New York: Macmillan, 1967), p. 36.

10. See Alain Robbe-Grillet's comments on *Waiting for Godot* in *Critique* 9 (February 1953), pp. 108–14.

11. Citations in the text from *Endgame* are from the Grove Press edition.

12. Citations in the text from Chekhov are from *The Plays of Anton Chekhov*, trans. Paul Schmidt.

13. Goodman, p. 212.

14. Citations in the text from *The Coast of Utopia* are from the Grove Press edition (New York, 2002).

15. Citations from *A Streetcar Named Desire* are from the Signet edition (New York, 1974).

16. Personal communication from the playwright, October 2000.

17. Quoted by Brater, *The Essential Samuel Beckett*, p. 136.

18. Citations in the text from *Waiting for Godot* are from the Grove Press edition.

19. Brater, *The Essential Samuel Beckett*, p. 82.

20. Atlas is the son of Japhetos; Beckett corrected the error. See Ackerley and Gontarski, p. 28.

21. See Michael Worton, '*Waiting for Godot* and *Endgame*: Theatre as Text', in *The Cambridge Companion to Samuel Beckett*, ed. John Pilling (Cambridge: Cambridge University Press, 1994), p. 67.

22. Citations in the text from *Playing for Time* are from *Arthur Miller Plays: Two* (London: Methuen Drama, 2009).

23. See Brater, *The Essential Samuel Beckett*, p. 136.

24. Ibid., p. 78.

25. Beckett's final stage direction in *Waiting for Godot*.

26. Joyce, *Ulysses*, p. 381.

27. Duckworth, p. 68.

28. 'Less is more' is Beckett's note to *That Time*. See Ruby Cohn, *Just Play: Beckett's Theater* (Princeton: Princeton University Press, 1980), p. 172.

29. Citations in my text from *Angels in America* are from the Theater Communications Group edition (New York, 1993).

30. Citations in my text from *Rosencrantz and Guildenstern Are Dead* are from the Grove Press edition (New York, 1967).

31. Arthur Miller, *Timebends: A Life* (New York: Grove Press, 1987), p.180.

32. *Worstward Ho*, p. 7.

33. See Book I, line 462, of *The Aeneid*; translated as lines 628–9 by Robert Fitzgerald, *The Aeneid* (New York: Vintage 1990), p. 20.

Notes to Addendum

1. For discussions of modernist and postmodernist perspectives, see Linda Hutcheon, *A Poetics of Postmodernism: History, Theory, Fiction* (London: Routledge, 1987); Frederic Jameson, *Postmodernism: The Cultural Logic of Late Capitalism* (Durham: Duke University Press, 1991); Marjorie Perloff, ed., *Postmodern Genres* (Norman: University of Oklahoma Press, 1988); Deborah R. Geis, *Postmodern Theatric[ks]: Monologue in Contemporary American Drama* (Ann Arbor: University of Michigan Press, 1993); H. Porter Abbott, 'Late Modernism: Samuel Beckett and the Art of the Oeuvre', in Enoch Brater and Ruby Cohn, eds., *Around the Absurd: Essays on Modern and Postmodern Drama* (Ann Arbor: University of Michigan Press, 1990), pp. 75–96; and Begam, *Samuel Beckett and the End of Modernity*.

2. Maurice Beebe, 'What Modernism Was', *Journal of Modern Literature* (July 1974), p. 1065.

3. Cleanth Brooks, *The Well Wrought Urn: Studies in the Structure of Poetry* (New York: Harcourt, Brace & World, 1947).

4. Enoch Brater, 'The Empty Can: Samuel Beckett and Andy Warhol', *Journal of Modern Literature* (July 1974), pp. 1255–64.

5. See Harold Rosenberg, *The Anxious Object: Art Today and Its Audience* (New York: Horizon, 1964); and *Watt*, p. 75.

6. Quoted by Brater in *Why Beckett*, p. 110.

7. *Footfalls*, p. 241.

8. Ibid., p. 243.

9. See H. Porter Abbott, 'A Grammar for Being Elsewhere', *Journal of Modern Literature* (February 1977), pp. 39–46. Special Beckett Number.

10. Brienza, p. 88.

11. Samuel Beckett, *Worstward Ho*, pp. 28, 29; and Samuel Beckett, *what is the word*, in *As the Story Was Told: Uncollected and Late Prose*, p. 132. For 'nothingness / in words enclose', see the Addenda to *Watt*, p. 247.

12. Beckett used the phrase 'work-in-regress' on a postcard addressed to Ruby Cohn on 14 December 1971 (see also p. 177, n. 23). Since the early 1970s there have been a number of useful studies linking Beckett's work to the non-literary arts. See in particular Oppenheim, *The Painted Word*; Mary Bryden, ed., *Samuel Beckett and Music*; and Oppenheim, ed., *Samuel Beckett and the Arts: Music, Visual Arts, and Non-Print Media*.

13. See *Eh Joe* in *The Collected Shorter Plays of Samuel Beckett*, p. 203; and *Worstward Ho*, p. 43.
14. See . . . *but the clouds* . . . and *Ohio Impromptu*, pp. 261, 285; and *Worstward Ho*, p. 47.

INDEX